STOP OVERTHINKING

Turn Off your Intensive & Negative Thoughts: How to Declutter and Unfu*k your Mind, discover Fast Success Habits and start Thinking Positively. Slow down the Brain and Be Yourself.

1

Stop Overthinking

"Don't get too deep, it leads to overthinking, and overthinking leads to problems that don't even exist in the first place."

– Jayson Engay

Table of content

General Introduction 13

Chapter:1 17

What the Symptoms of Over-Thinking 17

You're Less Creative.. 20

Your Sleep May Take A Hit 22

Your Appetite Might Change 23

Chapter:2 28

Powerful Methods To Declutter Your Mind And Fill It Back
Up With Healthy, Productive Habits And Encouragement.. 28

A: Focused Deep Breathing............................... 38

B: Learn Meditation 39

C: Reframing Negative Thoughts...................... 39

D: Teach Your Old Mind New Tricks.................. 40

E: Identify Your Core Values............................. 40

F: Practice Empathic Listening........................ 41

Chapter :3 42

How to Challenge Your Thoughts? 42

Where Do Negative Thoughts Come From? 42

The Types of Negative Thinking 43

How to Challenge Our Negative Thinking? 50

A: Stand Up to Your Critical Inner Voice 56

B: Think About Where These Voices Come From.............56

C: Stand Up to Your Critical Inner Voice 57

D: Use Mindfulness to Choose Your Thoughts...............58

E: Shift the Way You See Problems...........................59

Chapter:4 60

Definitions and Examples of Positive Thinking 60

Understanding Positive Thinking and Self-Talk...............61

The Health Benefits of Positive Thinking 62

Identifying Negative Thinking 63

Practicing Positive Thinking Every Day 66

A Perspective Is Useful If It: 67

Chapter:5 68

How to Recognize Negative Thought Patterns 68

Judgment 72

Impression Formation 73

Fundamental Attribution Error 74

Stereotyping 76

Gullibility 77

Memory 78

Misinformation Effect...78

In Witness of Events..79

In Recall of Past Public Events 80

Degree of Enhanced Memory 82

Interpersonal Benefits 83

Intergroup Discrimination 83

Communication 84

Self-Disclosure 86

What Causes GAD? 91

How Is GAD Treated? 92

Psychotherapy 92

Medication 92

Benzodiazepines 93

What Is It Like to Have GAD? 94

Following Are 3 Negative Thinking Patterns to Avoid—And
What to Do Instead: 96

1. Negative Rumination 96

2. Overthinking 98

3. Cynical Hostility 99

But It Doesn't Have To. 101

Negative Thinking Gets Wired Into Your Brain 102

The Most Common Negative Thinking Traps 103

Challenge Your Thinking 105

Is Thought Helping or Hurting? 106

What Counts as Negative Thinking? 108

What Are the Causes of Negative Thinking? 109

How to Stop Negative Thinking Once and For All? 111

Chapter:6 114

How to Slow Down Thought Momentum...................................114

What Feelings in You Right Now? 119

Happy in Five Minutes..122

Chapter:7 124

Why Nighttime Is the Worst Time for Overthinking............124

Classification 124

Cause..125

Treatment 127

Posttraumatic Stress Disorder 128

Epidemiology 129

Signs and Symptoms...131

Consequences 132

Content of Idiopathic Nightmares 133

Criteria 133

Causes...134

Assessment 136

Comorbidity..137

Treatment 138

Pharmacological Treatments 141

Epidemiology 142

Research..143

Nightmare Pictures...146

Why Two?..147

Removed Sections 148

Etymology 148

Folk Remedies 149

Categorization... 149

Nightmares: One of The Bodies Defense Mechanisms? 156

Dying in A Dream?.. 157

Rewrite Paragraph 158

Ghost?.. 159

Multivitamins May Be Causing Your Sleep Problems...... 162

Chapter:8 165

How Neuroplasticity Can Help Overcome Overthinking 165

Getting Stuck in Anxiety... 166

Chapter :9 167

How to Declutter Your Environment to Reflect the Positive Changes You're Making in Your Life.................................. 167

Your Workspace 167

Your Bedroom 168

Your Closet... 168

Your Desktop.. 169

Your Social Media Feeds 169

Your Thoughts 170

Chapter:10... 171

How to Address Information Overload in Your Life............ 171

Manage Your Information 171

Get Everyone Involved 172

Keep It Simple.. 172

Clear Your Mind... 173

Set Limits.. 174

Prepare for The Next Day 175

Conclusion...177

General Introduction

Overthinking is considered as an excessive amount of unnecessary thoughts. Overthinking can be associated with anxiety. To prevent or treat overthinking disorder and anxiety, knots of negative emotions have to be disentangled. Positive emotions such as love, joy, gratitude balance with the intellectual capacity of mind so that overthinking does not happen all the time. People that have enough positive emotions can better deal with everyday difficulties and can also be more prepared for stressful events.

The brain is very resilient and does not snap away like a tightened string or burst like an over-inflated balloon.

The more we think, the more the brain rewires itself to strengthen those circuits involved in thinking. For example, if one is thinking a lot about how to solve a mathematical problem, the synapses of the concerned circuits are strengthened so that our skill in solving mathematical problems is enhanced. The more we use our brains for learning a skill, the easier it becomes to execute. It is dependent on the remarkable ability of the brain to rewire itself and goes by the name neural plasticity. As far as the brain is concerned the dictim is - Use it or Lose it.

o overcome overthinking; Pittman recommends you replace the thought. "Telling yourself not to have a certain thought is not the way to not have the thought," she says. "You need to replace the thought." What if she were to tell you to stop thinking about pink elephants? What are you going to think about? That's right: pink elephants. If you don't want to think about a pink elephant, conjure up an image of, say, a tortoise. "Maybe a big tortoise is holding a rose in its mouth as it crawls," says Pittman. "You're not thinking about pink elephants now."

Talk yourself out of it by noticing when you're stuck in your head. You can take your overthinking habit if you can start taking a grip on your self-talk — that inner voice that provides a running monologue throughout the day and even into the night.

14

If overthinking is ruining your life, and if you think you may be spiraling into depression because of your thoughts, it pays to get professional help

Chapter:1

What the Symptoms of Over-Thinking

Overthinking Disorder doesn't exist. There are many different kinds of anxiety disorders where an individual engages in overthinking or rumination, but there is not a disorder. When an individual cannot stop obsessing and worrying over things it can interfere with your quality of life.

You may be wondering "what conditions cause overthinking?" Some mental health diagnoses where a person can't stop their brain from rumination are PTSD, trauma, agoraphobia, panic disorder, selective mutism, separation anxiety disorder, social anxiety disorder, phobias, substance-induced anxiety disorders, or it could potentially be a symptom of some other illness.

When it comes to anxiety disorders, many of them have to overthink as a symptom. For example, a person with panic disorder might ruminate and overthink when they are going to have a panic attack again. They obsess over something that could trigger their attack.

"[It's] the process of constantly analyzing and anguishing over one's thoughts," Huttman told MyDomaine. "It may include rumination, in which an individual is stuck mentally rehashing their past or present decisions and/or actions."

Overthinking is very common and may be caused by self-doubt; self-esteem issues; concern about repeating past patterns about prior bad experiences; traumatic experiences; according to Huttman. Overthinking makes it harder to enjoy life and can impact emotional regulation too.

"Overthinking is the process of constantly analyzing and anguishing over one's thoughts. It may include rumination, in which an individual is stuck mentally rehashing their past or present decisions and/or actions."

"In a very general and non-scientific sense, people with a Type A personality are more likely to be more ambitious, competitive, and intense," Huttman says. "Those with a personality are alleged to be more relaxed—less frantic and reactive. Twould certainly be more likely to engage in overthinking."

If you have a Type A personality, we feel you, but you're by no means a lost cause. While overthinking may feel out of your control, there are some steps you can take to turn things around today.

"He discusses the research of a mindfulness-based stress reduction program (MBSR) and guides the reader on how to meditate, control stress/worry thoughts, and become present at the moment," Huttman says.

The MBSR program was founded by Kabat-Zinn and is based around mindfulness meditation. Several studies have found the practice to be helpful.

Overthinking creates so many options, choices, and scenarios that you end up unable to make a decision — a concept called analysis paralysis.

"You could get stuck in potential consequences that may not even happen, just worrying about certain outcomes, and that can paralyze us or freeze us from taking an action," said Rajita Sinha, the director of the Yale Stress Center.

If you don't try things, you don't fail, which may be a potential concern but you also don't succeed, she added. When you do finally move forward with a decision, you might wind up making the wrong one because you got so mixed up by all the competing thoughts.

"Your gut feeling or instinct gets overridden because you have so much other input … and you maybe end up not making the choices that are right for you at that moment," said Laura Price, a clinical assistant professor in the department of psychiatry at NYU Langone Health.

You're Less Creative

A study from the U.K. discovered that when certain parts of your brain and cognitive processes are quiet, you're more creative. Overthinking — which can lead to a "mental rut," as the study notes — can essentially cause you to get stuck and run out of ideas or new solutions. While some overthinking can lead to fresh, new ideas, it can also backfire and create mental roadblocks that make it challenging to think outside the box.

Another study from Stanford came to the same conclusion. While hooked up to magnetic resonance imaging machines (MRIs), participants were asked to draw a series of images — some easy to illustrate, some difficult. The more difficult the images were to draw, the more the participants had to think, and the less creative their drawings were. On the flip side, the less thought involved, the more creative the drawings were.

In short, too much thinking seems to put a cap on creativity.

Your energy levels might drop

It takes a lot of mental energy to overthink. Your brain is generating so many different thoughts and scenarios that aren't going toward anything productive.

"Mental energy without any sort of physical outlet absolutely can make it fatiguing and make it feel like you're exhausted because you spent so much time in your head," Price said.

Spiegel added that when we overthink and stress ourselves out, our bodies produce cortisol, the stress hormone. Over time, the constant release of cortisol can be depleting and cause burnout.

"It's like running your car in the wrong gear. Your motor's running but you're not getting very far," Spiegel said.

Your Sleep May Take A Hit

Lots of overthinkers struggle with falling asleep, shuffling through thoughts rather than shutting down and getting some shut-eye.

Your body needs to get into a state of calm to sleep — your heart rate needs to go down, as does your blood pressure and breathing. Overanalyzing can be arousing, especially when the thoughts are more anxious. This can pull you out of the soothing state your body needs to be in for sleep, according to Spiegel.

And once your sleep starts suffering, it's easy to get stuck in a nasty whirlwind of exhaustion and sleep deprivation.

"If you don't sleep as well, you have less energy, you get less exercise, then you sleep even worse," Spiegel said.

Your Appetite Might Change

Overthinking can have a profound impact on people's appetites. For some, it can suppress appetite, and for others, it can boost it — which is more common.

Spiegel calls this "worry eating," and said people do it because it can be distracting or even soothing. Many people tend to go for the tastiest and unhealthiest things when they're stressed, Spiegel said, noting there's a reason high-fat, sugary foods are called "comfort foods."

Additionally, cortisol — that stress hormone we talked about earlier — increases your appetite along with your motivation to eat, according to Harvard University

The first step is to notice that you're overthinking and become aware of what's going on. According to Sinha, one way to think about it is if you have more than three potential, or "what if," scenarios, you're thinking about it too much.

Next, you want to find a way to distract yourself and get into your physical body to free up your cognitive systems (think to go for a jog or trying yoga). Price practices diaphragmatic breathing, or deep belly breathing, with her patients. This helps lower your heart rate, slow your breathing and get in touch with your body — which, in turn, clears your head.

She also recommended using a worry log: 20 minutes before bed, write down a list of everything you're worried about or have to do.

"The process of writing it down — not typing, but writing — has a processing effect to your brain to help get it out of that spin cycle," Price said.

Talking to a therapist, friend or loved one can also give you a fresh perspective and realize that something that seems terrible or complex isn't so complicated after all.

Lastly, mindfulness or meditation can also help you reset and declutter your mind, according to Spiegel, though this will likely take a bit of practice and patience.

Not only are they anxious, they now have meta-anxiety, which is anxiety about being anxious. Overthinking their panic attack made it feel more daunting.

Overthinking is common. You don't have to have an anxiety disorder to engage in constant rumination. You might say it's part of the human condition. We all overthink things at times: You may be overly concerned with what you said or did to somebody. You may be worried about performing at school or work. You might be concerned about how others see you. These are all examples of how you might engage in overthinking.

Many people are familiar with the term anxiety disorder (and millions of Americans suffer from some sort of anxiety disorder every day), but we tend to overlook a major symptom of anxiety disorders, which is overthinking.

The definition of overthinking is to ruminate or obsess about something. A lot of people, when hearing this definition, might believe they are overthinkers. Who doesn't go a single day without overthinking something? We wonder if we're making the right choices from small things like picking the fastest route on our commute that morning or selecting the right restaurant for dinner to things like our children's wellbeing and our family's safety and security. But that's normal. It's common to worry and overthink to some extent.

However, harmful effects are overthinking can have on a person mentally and emotionally. When overthinking as it pertains to an anxiety disorder, it would be excessive thoughts about something that causes one anxiety, stress, fear, or dread. It's not just thinking too much about something-it's obsessing about something so much that it affects one's ability to function in their life.

When you wander or worry about yourself, your life, your family, your friends, or anything else and you don't have an overthinking issue, whatever you're pondering about I worries you for a while, then after a short period, you go on with your day. You continue worrying at times, but you don't constantly ruminate. You don't find the worry interfering with the rest of your life. With overthinking as the result of an anxiety disorder, however, the worry is all the person can think about and even though they may not obsess about the same thing all the time, they're always concerned about something.

Chapter:2

Powerful Methods To Declutter Your Mind And Fill It Back Up With Healthy, Productive Habits And Encouragement.

If you're not paying attention, your mind operates on autopilot and meanders through a landscape of mental clutter that doesn't always serve you well.

Our powerful brains are constantly processing all sorts of experiences and analyzing them in the form of thoughts. Thoughts form what we perceive to be a reality.

We can control and direct our thoughts, but it often feels like our thoughts have minds of their own, controlling us and how we feel. Thinking is necessary for solving problems, analyzing, making decisions, and planning, but in between the times of proactive mental endeavors, the mind roams like a wild monkey, dragging you through the brambles of rumination and negativity.

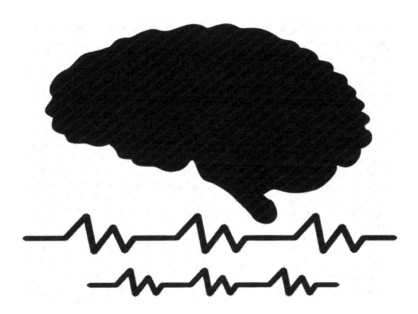

Thinking about something in endless circles — is exhausting.

While everyone overthinks a few things once in a while, chronic over-thinkers spend most of their waking time ruminating, which puts pressure on themselves. They then mistake that pressure to be stress.

"There are people who have levels of overthinking that are just pathological," says clinical psychologist Catherine Pittman, an associate professor in the psychology department at Saint Mary's College in Notre Dame, Indiana.

"But the average person also just tends to overthink things." Pittman is also the author of "Rewire Your Anxious Brain: How to Use the Neuroscience of Fear to End Anxiety, Panic, and Worry."

Overthinking can take many forms: endlessly deliberating when making a decision (and then questioning the decision), attempting to read minds, trying to predict the future, reading into the smallest of details, etc.

People who overthink consistently run commentaries in their heads, criticizing and picking apart what they said and did yesterday, terrified that they look bad — and fretting about a terrible future that might await them

'What ifs' and 'should' dominate their thinking, as if an invisible jury is sitting in judgment on their lives. And they also agonies over what to post online because they are deeply concerned about how other people will interpret their posts and updates.

They don't sleep well because ruminating and worrying keep them awake at night. "Ruminators repetitively go over events, asking big questions: Why did that happen? What does it mean?" adds Susan Nolen-Hoeksema, the chair of the department of psychology at Yale University and the author of Women Who Think Too Much: How to Break Free of Overthinking and Reclaim Your Life. "But they never find any answers."

If you consistently focus on ruminating and make it a habit, And the more you do it, the harder it is to stop. Clinical psychologist Helen Ode's sky, Psy. D., shares some insight. "So often people confuse overthinking with problem-solving," says Ode's sky, the author of "Stop Anxiety from Stopping You."

"But what ends up happening is we just sort of go in a loop," Ode's sky says. "We're not solving a problem."

Overthinking is destructive and mentally draining. It can make you feel like you're stuck in one place, and if you don't act, it can greatly impact your day-to-day life. It can quickly put your health and total well-being at risk. Rumination makes you more susceptible to depression and anxiety.

Many people overthink because they are scared of the future, and what could potentially go wrong. "Because we feel vulnerable about the future, we keep trying to solve problems in our head," says David Carbonell, a clinical psychologist and author of "The Worry Trick: How Your Brain Tricks You into Expecting the Worst and What You Can Do About It."

Extreme overthinking can easily sap your sense of control over your life. It robs us of active participation in everything around us.

"Chronic worriers show an increased incidence of coronary problems and suppressed immune functioning. Dwelling on the past or the future also takes us away from the present, rendering us unable to complete the work currently on our plates. If you ask ruminators how they are feeling, none will say "happy." Most feel miserable," says Nicholas Petrie, a senior faculty member at the Center for Creative Leadership.

Overthinking can trap the brain in a worry cycle. When ruminating becomes as natural as breathing, you need to quickly deal with it and find a solution to it.

"When an unpleasant event puts us in a despondent mood, it's easier to recall other times when we've felt terrible. That can set the stage for a ruminator to work herself into a downward spiral," writes Amy Maclin of Real Simple.

How to defeat this pattern of thinking and win your life back

Chronic worrying is not permanent. It's a mental habit that can be broken. You can train your brain to look at life from a different perspective.

To overcome overthinking, Pittman recommends you replace the thought. "Telling yourself not to have a certain thought is not the way to not have the thought," she says. "You need to replace the thought." What if she were to tell you to stop thinking about pink elephants? What are you going to think about? That's right: pink elephants. If you don't want to think about a pink elephant, conjure up an image of, say, a tortoise. "Maybe a big tortoise is holding a rose in its mouth as it crawls," says Pittman. "You're not thinking about pink elephants now."

Talk yourself out of it by noticing when you're stuck in your head. You can tame your overthinking habit if you can start taking a grip on your self-talk — that inner voice that provides a running monologue throughout the day and even into the night.

"You can cultivate a little psychological distance by generating other interpretations of the situation, which makes your negative thoughts less believable," says Bruce Hubbard, the director of the Cognitive Health Group and an adjunct assistant professor of psychology and education at Columbia University. This is called cognitive restructuring.

Ask yourself — What's the probability that what I'm scared of will happen? If the probability is low, what are some more likely outcomes?

If it's a problem you keep ruminating about, rephrase the issue to reflect the positive outcome you're looking for," suggests Nolen-Hoeksema.

"Instead of "I'm stuck in my career," tell yourself or better still write, "I want a job where I feel more engaged." Then make a plan to expand your skills, network, and look for opportunities for a better career.

Find a constructive way of processing any worries or negative thoughts, says Honey. "Write your thoughts down in a journal every night before bed or first thing in the morning — they don't have to be in any order. Do a 'brain dump' of everything on your mind onto the page. Sometimes that can afford a sense of relief," recommends Honey Lancaster-James, a psychologist.

You can also control your ruminating habit by connecting with your senses. Begin to notice what you can hear, see, smell, taste, and feel.

The idea is to reconnect with your immediate world and everything around you. When you begin to notice, you spend less time in your head.

You can also notice your overthinking habit and talk yourself out of it. Becoming self-aware can help you take control.

"Pay a little more attention," says Carbonell. "Say something like: I'm feeling kind of anxious and uncomfortable. Where am I? Am I all in my head? Maybe I should go take a walk around the block and see what happens."

Recognize your brain is in overdrive or ruminating mode, and then try to snap out of it immediately. Or better still, distract yourself and redirect your attention to something else that requires focus.

"If you need to interrupt and replace hundreds of times a day, it will stop fast, probably within a day," says Dr. Margaret Weherenberg, a psychologist and author of the 10 Best-Ever Anxiety Management Techniques. "Even if the switch is simply to return attention to the task at hand, it should be a decision to change ruminative thoughts."

It takes practice, but with time, you will be able to easily recognize when you are worrying unnecessarily and choose instead, to do something in real life rather than spending a lot of time in your head.

For example, convert, "I can't believe this happened" to "What can I do to prevent it from happening again?" or convert "I don't have good friends!" to "What steps could I take to deepen the friendships I have and find new ones?" recommends Ryan Howes, Ph.D.

Don't get lost in thoughts about what you could have, would have, and should have done differently. Mental stress can seriously impact your quality of life.

An overactive mind can make life miserable. Learning how to stop spending time in your head is one of the greatest gifts you can give yourself.

Like all habits, changing your destructive thought patterns can be a challenge, but it's not impossible. With practice, you can train your brain to perceive things differently and reduce the stress of overthinking.

If overthinking is ruining your life, and if you think you may be spiraling into depression because of your thoughts, it pays to get professional help.

Your constant inner dialog distracts you from what is happening around you, right here and now. It causes you to miss valuable experiences and sabotages the joy of the present moment.

Fortunately, you can control your "monkey mind" and become more mindful of the present moment.

As you learn to manage your thoughts, you can also apply to declutter to other areas of your life to support a more mindful and conscious way of life.

Let's take a look at some simple actions you can take to declutter your mind, your relationships, and your life.

A: Focused Deep Breathing

A change in breathing is often the first sign that our thoughts are overwhelming and stressful.

When we feel anxious, depressed, rushed, or upset, we may experience rapid breathing or shortness of breath.

You may not pay much attention to your breathing and your posture, but by simply becoming more aware of how you breathe, you foster a calmer state of body and mind.

B: Learn Meditation

If you've never practiced meditation or you're not familiar with it, you might be put off by the idea of sitting quietly in the lotus position and emptying your mind.

The benefits of meditating translate to your daily life, helping you control worry and overthinking, and providing a host of health benefits.

C: Reframing Negative Thoughts

Critical thinking gives us the ability to solve problems quickly and effectively.

Creative thinking allows us to develop original, diverse, and elaborate ideas and connections.

But it's the uninvited negative thinking that clutters our minds and often drains our enthusiasm for life.

Many people go through their entire lives victimized by their negative thoughts.

They feel they have no control of what thoughts take up residence in their brains—and worse, they believe the "voices" in their heads that tell them the sky is falling.

D: Teach Your Old Mind New Tricks

You will always struggle with some amount of negative thinking. You can't overcome millions of years of evolutionary wiring through sheer willpower.

However, you can manage the pain by being more proactive in what you allow to remain in your thoughts.

Interrupting cluttered thinking is only part of the process of retraining your brain and learning to disassociate from negative thoughts.

Your mind abhors a vacuum, so you need to fill the void with constructive thought so you don't career back into old patterns.

E: Identify Your Core Values

One of the challenges of modern living is figuring out what's truly important and differentiating those things from the obligations that seem important at first, but don't matter when you take the time to examine them.

If you're like most people, you might find that it's increasingly difficult to minimize, organize, or bypass the deluge of information you encounter regularly.

F: Practice Empathic Listening.

Active music is a willingness to step outside of your distracted mind and listen to the other person's words in a non-judgmental way.

You remain completely attentive to what the person is saying. Avoid interrupting, even when you have something important to add.

Also, ask open-ended questions that invite more from the speaker. Avoid coming to premature conclusions or offering solutions. Be sure to reflect the speaker what you heard them say.

Chapter :3

How to Challenge Your Thoughts?

Contestant negative thinking (also known as rumination) isn't healthy, and overcoming it is a process that takes conscious awareness and a committed effort. Negative or unwanted thoughts undermine your self-confidence and leave you plagued with insecurities. Rather than allowing yourself to be distracted by what isn't, you have to learn to focus on what is — and learn how to live a happier life by understanding your negative emotions and how you can reframe them.

Where Do Negative Thoughts Come From?

Negative thinking is fear-based, meaning it stems from our insecurities and those things in life which wounded us or made us hesitant. We are born as a blank slate and form our beliefs and opinions over time, based on the examples set by our caretakers and the experiences that comprise our lives.

All of these things come together to form the foundation of how we interact with the world, and it is through these experiences that we form our ideas of self and ability. Negative thinking can develop in a lot of secret and hidden parts of ourselves, but it's our responsibility to dig deep and try to understand where it comes from. While our experiences can contribute to our negative patterns of thinking, the quality and state of the brain can contribute as well, hindering our positivity with vengeful mental illnesses like depression and anxiety.

The Types of Negative Thinking

Negative thinking is also referred to as cognitive distortion in the psych world. These cognitive distortions are simply how our mind convinces us of something that isn't quite true. These inaccurate thoughts reinforce our negative thinking and keep us stuck. To overcome them, you have to understand them.

1. Polarization

When we trap ourselves in a polarized way of thinking, we start to see things as only "black or white". Polarized thinking means all or nothing; it means having to be perfect or being a complete failure. There is no middle ground when our thinking is polar. It's impossible to compromise with ourselves or anyone else for that matter.

Those with polarized thinking place people and situations in either/or categories. There is no shade of grey when it comes to the way they view the world, and even the most complex of circumstances is meaningless to them. There are only extremes when everything is either one thing or another. One of the most toxic forms of negative thinking can also be one of the most difficult to accept, reframe and overcome.

2. Filtering

Those who filter their thinking magnify the negative details they find in situations or people. Rather than seeing the good in a situation, they filter out all the positive and focus — with a magnifying glass — on all the negatives. They're fixated by their disappointment and they expect that same fixation from the people around them.

These are the people that pick out a single, unpleasant detail and pick at it until it's a major irritation. They like to dwell on things that make them unhappy because it gives them a sense of the power of justification in their victimhood. Their reality is dark and it's distorted. Being around them feels like an energy-suck.

3. The Heavenly Rewarder

While it is often overlooked, thinking (obsessively) that you will be rewarded for misery or self-sacrifice is an extremely dangerous and negative way of thinking. This is known as Heaven's Reward Fallacy, and it is the false belief that a person's sacrifice and self-denial will pay off to some omnipotent force that's keeping score for everyone involved.

Thinking in this way relies on the fallacy of fairness or the idea that in a fair world those who work the hardest and sacrifice the most will get "redeemed". When they don't get the payoff, they built up in their minds, those who think in this way can become bitter in their disappointments.

4. Emotional Reasoning

This distortion of emotional reasoning is when a person believes that their feelings are automatically right and true — no matter what. The problem with this, of

45

course, is that (as humans) our emotions are not always justified and often come from a place that is different from our actual outside circumstances. Emotions are extremely strong and can overrule our logic when we don't take the time to understand them and address them rationally.

When our emotions take over entirely, this is emotional reasoning, and it blots out all rationality or logic we might have seen from a different perspective. Those who engage in emotional reasoning are not people who can be reasoned with. This is because emotions do not come only from our brains; they also come from our hearts, our souls and our past experiences.

5. Personalization

When you believe that everything others do is a reaction to you, you are personalizing your thinking. This type of thinking takes you to an obsessive place, where you start to compare yourself to others in a way that is not only unhealthy but self-defeating as well.

Those who engage in personalized thinking often see themselves as the cause of everything bad, even if they weren't the cause of it. Sometimes, this kind of self-flagellation can stem from a place of low self-esteem, but beware: it can also come from a need for attention or a need to manipulate the emotions of others.

6. Overgeneralization

This is a common cognitive distortion and one in which a person comes to a general conclusion based on a single incident or a single piece of evidence. It doesn't matter to this person if the evidence is flimsy or lacking invalidity when a bad thing happens once, they expect it to happen over and over again.

A single event becomes a never-ending pattern of self-defeat. Their insecurities cause them to throw in the towel before they've ever really given themselves a chance to begin. Overgeneralization is a cycle that has to be broken, lest it overcomes us and skews the way we view ourselves and the world and people around us.

7. Catastrophizing

People who catastrophize expect a disaster to strike — no matter what. This type of distortion is also known as magnifying and is a bit like filtering.

Those who engage in this type of negative thinking can simply hear about a problem and quickly build a catastrophe on top of their what-if's. They always imagine the absolute worst and no matter what assurances they receive; they just know that only bad is going to happen.

8. Jumping to Conclusions

Jumping to conclusions occurs when someone believes they know the thoughts and feelings of others around them better than they do. This type of thinking can result in fortune-telling or holding grudges. There's a whole array of toxic attitudes and behaviors it inspires. One thing is certain, though: those who employ this type of thinking have a hard time focusing on anything other than negative outcomes.

9. Blaming

This type of cognitive distortion involves holding others responsible for the things we feel uncomfortable embracing responsibility for.

When a person engages in blaming, they find it hard to hold themselves responsible for the decisions or actions that led them to a certain point; or, conversely, they can blame themselves for everything and internalize a self-hatred that is <u>corrosive</u> to their wellbeing.

10. Global Labeling

Global labeling is a massive generalization that focuses on one or two qualities or judgments about ourselves or other people. This extreme form of overgeneralization centers around attaching an unhealthy self-label rather than describing an error in the context of a given situation.

When we mislabel, we describe an event with language that is highly colored and emotionally loaded. Rather than accepting that we failed a single task, we label ourselves losers and start to form our personalities around those beliefs.

11. The fallacy of Change.

This is the belief that with enough outward pressure, you can change or control another person's behavior or choices. This extremely toxic sort of negative thinking is common in relationships with a high level of codependence or emotional dependency, and can also be seen commonly in those who have experienced heartbreak or trauma in the past.

12. The Should As

While this might sound like a great 80's girl-band name, it's a common cognitive distortion and one many of us engage in from time to time. The Should as is should statements, which often turn into an ironclad list of rules on how you and every other person should behave.

When people break the rules, those who engage in this type of negative thinking see them instantly as enemies; transgressors that cannot be redeemed. Thinking in a "shoulda" mentality will cause you to believe that you are trying to motivate yourself, but in reality, you're just building up more walls. The emotional consequences of this type of thinking always wind up being guilt, something most of us could do without.

How to Challenge Our Negative Thinking?

Our negative thoughts can seem scary or intimidating, but they can be tackled and redirected with a little understanding and know-how. Once you've learned how to identify your manner and patterns of negative thinking, you can start to reframe those thoughts by challenging them and the beliefs that reinforce them.

1. Recognize the Thought-Loop Before It Starts.

Once you know what kind of negative thinking you commonly engage in, you can start to recognize the triggers that bring on those defeating thought-loops. Stop the negative thoughts before they start and be honest about what brings about the worst reactions in you.

Try to eliminate the factors in your environment that contribute to your negative beliefs and feelings and replace them with more positive factors that can help you channel that energy into something more efficient.

2. Ask Yourself Probing Questions.

Just as you would challenge any would-be politician, challenge your thinking and beliefs with probing questions.

When you find yourself slipping down the rabbit hole of negative feedback loops, ask yourself the hard questions and try to get to the bottom of why you feel that way. Question the experiences you've had and the assumptions you make; question your reactions and the way you view the people involved in the situation.

Only when you learn how to question your emotions and thoughts can you get to the root of them. Finding solutions isn't always easy. It takes time to get the answers we need from the self. Be patient and accept that any change worth having taken time. You can do this, but it's going to take some brutal honesty.

3. Distract Yourself.

Negative thoughts don't seem to happen one at a time, they seem to happen in a cluster or a swarm. When the negativity gets too strong for you to handle, switch off for a little while and give yourself the distance you need to calm down with a little distraction.

Get yourself stuck into an activity that takes your mind off of the bad thoughts and redirects your energy into something more positive. Talking to someone is a good distraction, as well as going on a hike or traveling somewhere new.

There is no one-size-fits-all solution when it comes to distracting ourselves from bad thoughts, just try to find something that speaks to your passions in a way that makes you feel happy again.

4. Replace the Negative with Something Rational.

Rather than thinking about what you aren't, try thinking about what you are. Negative thoughts are often irrational and based on distortions of reality. When we replace those thoughts with positive ones (which are based on real, verifiable strengths or virtues that we have) we can combat the negative thoughts more productively.

Instead of thinking, "I'm ugly," look through flattering pictures or focus on the parts of your body that you adore. Those are things that exist right here, right now. They are real things that we can celebrate, but we have to have the courage to see them.

5. Release Your Judgements.

More often than not, our negative thoughts are judgment; a judgment of ourselves, a judgment of others. We are one judgey species.

Rather than comparing yourself to others or constantly comparing your life against some ridiculous ideal, let go of your hang-ups and be more at ease with who you are and what you have. You can take a break from your judgmental high horse by recognizing your reactions and observing them briefly before letting them go.

When you notice that you're judging yourself or someone else negatively — stop and try to look for something positive or redeeming that can help you see them (and yourself) in a different light.

6. Practice Gratitude.

Gratitude is one of the fastest and easiest ways to challenge and undo our negative thinking, but it can take a little time to get right and it always takes a bit of creativity.

Feeling grateful can have a big impact on your happiness and can seriously affect your positivity. Even when things are going wrong, looking for the silver lining can help you survive by helping you release all the old baggage that kept you feeling stuck and miserable.

Noticing things are going well makes it possible for you to stay present at the moment and overcome whatever obstacles life has to throw at you. Keeping a gratitude journal is a great way to start and writing just a few things in it each day is an easy way to get back in touch with the things that you're grateful for.

Putting it all together...

It's hard to reframe our negative thoughts and emotions, but it's not impossible. By getting real about who we are and what we want from life, we can unlock the skills that we need to redirect our negative thoughts and channel them into positive energies.

Learn to understand your negative thinking and the shape your most self-chat takes. Spend time with these thoughts and come up with healthy ways you can reshape them into attitudes and beliefs that are more in line with who you are at a core level. Living in the light and truth of our authentic selves is hard and it takes letting go of the baggage that has held us tied down all the years. Reframe your negative thinking and learn how to use it for good by asking yourself the tough questions and having the courage to take charge of your happiness.

A: Stand Up to Your Critical Inner Voice

The negative thinking, we all experience can be hard to label as the nasty and alien enemy it truly is. We can spend hours berating ourselves about details from our day without even realizing how unrealistic and cruel we are being. By identifying these thoughts and recognizing when they are triggered, we can challenge our critical inner voice and change our way of thinking. There are three important steps to standing up to this inner critic:

B: Think About Where These Voices Come From

When you become aware of the specific thoughts you have toward yourself or others, you may start to see a pattern. Do you often feel more critical of your spouse when he or she brings up a certain subject? Do you turn on yourself when you're talking to your kids, your parents, your boss, a sibling or your partner? Once you come to know the types of critical inner voices you're experiencing, you can think about the real source of these thoughts. You may be surprised to learn they have very little to do with you and your real feelings in your current life or the current situation. For example, did someone treat you like you were stupid or incapable as a child? Were you taught to fend for yourself or not to trust others? All kinds of attitudes your parents or important early caretakers had toward themselves and toward you can seep into your consciousness and manifest themselves as your critical inner voice. Understanding where these attitudes come from can help you to separate them from your real point of view while having more compassion for yourself.

C: Stand Up to Your Critical Inner Voice

Journaling is a very helpful way to track what your critical inner voice is telling you. One very helpful exercise Dr. Firestone recommends in Conquer Your Critical Inner Voice is to write down these "voices" or thoughts as "Your" statements instead of "I" statements. i.e. "You're so ugly" as opposed to "I'm so ugly." "I'm useless; I always mess up" becomes "you're useless; you always mess up." This small-seeming alteration helps you to view the voice as an enemy and to see where it may have originated from in your past. It also paves the way for you to then respond to these voices from a more realistic and compassionate perspective.

Dr. Firestone recommends that you write down or verbalize a reply to each of these thoughts the way a friend would talk to you, i.e. "I'm an attractive person with a lot to offer." "I'm valuable and competent in many ways." The idea of this exercise isn't to boost your ego. It is about taking on a more honest and kinder attitude toward yourself, the sort of attitude you'd have toward a really good friend.

D: Use Mindfulness to Choose Your Thoughts

One proven tool that is incredibly effective in helping people to choose their thoughts and stop overthinking is mindfulness. "Mindfulness is a way of connecting with your life, and it's something that doesn't involve a lot of energy," said mindfulness expert Dr. Jon Kabat-Zinn. "It involves a kind of cultivating attention in a particular way... It's paying attention, on purpose, in the present moment non-judgmentally as if your life depended on it."

E: Shift the Way You See Problems

Reflecting on an important decision before making it is usually a wise course of action. However, when we start ruminating on or overthinking an issue in a negative sense, it can lead us to feel stressed or paralyzed about taking action. If we find ourselves having an exaggerated focus on a specific problem, how we are viewing that problem matters a lot.

By accepting that we have a great deal of control over our circumstances, by seeing problems as challenges and committing to stay the course and work hard through these challenges, Dr. Maddi says we can each become much more resilient and successful in getting what we want in life.

Chapter:4

Definitions and Examples of Positive Thinking

Is your glass half-empty or half-full? How you answer this age-old question about positive thinking may reflect your outlook on life, your attitude toward yourself, and whether you're optimistic or pessimistic — and it may even affect your health.

Indeed, some studies show that personality traits such as optimism and pessimism can affect many areas of your health and well-being. The positive thinking that usually comes with optimism is a key part of effective stress management. And effective stress management is associated with many health benefits. If you tend to be pessimistic, don't despair — you can learn positive thinking skills.

Understanding Positive Thinking and Self-Talk

Positive thinking doesn't mean that you keep your head in the sand and ignore life's less pleasant situations. Positive thinking just means that you approach unpleasantness more positively and productively. You think the best is going to happen, not the worst.

Positive thinking often starts with self-talk. Self-talk is the endless stream of unspoken thoughts that run through your head. These automatic thoughts can be positive or negative. Some of your self-talk comes from logic and reason. Other self-talk may arise from misconceptions that you create because of a lack of information.

If the thoughts that run through your head are mostly negative, your outlook on life is more likely pessimistic. If your thoughts are mostly positive, you're likely an optimist — someone who practices positive thinking.

The Health Benefits of Positive Thinking

Researchers continue to explore the effects of positive thinking and optimism on health. Health benefits that positive thinking may provide include:

- Increased life span
- Lower rates of depression
- Lower levels of distress
- Greater resistance to the common cold
- Better psychological and physical well-being
- Better cardiovascular health and reduced risk of death from cardiovascular disease
- Better coping skills during hardships and times of stress

It's unclear why people who engage in positive thinking experience these health benefits. One theory is that having a positive outlook enables you to cope better with stressful situations, which reduces the harmful health effects of stress on your body.

It's also thought that positive and optimistic people tend to live healthier lifestyles — they get more physical activity, follow a healthier diet, and don't smoke or drink alcohol in excess.

Identifying Negative Thinking

Not sure if your self-talk is positive or negative? Some common forms of negative self-talk include:

Filtering. You magnify the negative aspects of a situation and filter out all of the positive ones. For example, you had a great day at work. You completed your tasks ahead of time and were complimented for doing a speedy and thorough job. That evening, you focus only on your plan to do even more tasks and forget about the compliments you received.

Personalizing. When something bad occurs, you automatically blame yourself. For example, you hear that an evening out with friends is canceled, and you assume that the change in plans is because no one wanted to be around you.

Catastrophizing. You automatically anticipate the worst. The drive-through coffee shop gets your order wrong and you automatically think that the rest of your day will be a disaster.

Polarizing. You see things only as either good or bad. There is no middle ground. You feel that you have to be perfect or you're a total failure.

Focusing on positive thinking

You can learn to turn negative thinking into positive thinking. The process is simple, but it does take time and practice — you're creating a new habit, after all. Here are some ways to think and behave more positively and optimistically:

Identify areas to change. If you want to become more optimistic and engage in more positive thinking, first identify areas of your life that you usually think negatively about, whether it's work, your daily commute or a relationship. You can start small by focusing on one area to approach more positively.

Check yourself. Periodically during the day, stop and evaluate what you're thinking. If you find that your thoughts are mainly negative, try to find a way to put a positive spin on them.

Be open to humor. Give yourself permission to smile or laugh, especially during difficult times. Seek humor in everyday happenings. When you can laugh at life, you feel less stressed.

Follow a healthy lifestyle. Aim to exercise for about 30 minutes on most days of the week. You can also break it up into 10-minute chunks of time during the day. Exercise can positively affect mood and reduce stress. Follow a healthy diet to fuel your mind and body. And learn techniques to manage stress.

Surround yourself with positive people. Make sure those in your life are positive, supportive people you can depend on to give helpful advice and feedback. Negative people may increase your stress level and make you doubt your ability to manage stress in healthy ways.

Practice positive self-talk. Start by following one simple rule: Don't say anything to yourself that you wouldn't say to anyone else. Be gentle and encouraging with yourself. If a negative thought enters your mind, evaluate it rationally and respond with affirmations of what is good about you. Think about things you're thankful for in your life.

Practicing Positive Thinking Every Day

If you tend to have a negative outlook, don't expect to become an optimist overnight. But with practice, eventually, your self-talk will contain less self-criticism and more self-acceptance. You may also become less critical of the world around you.

When your state of mind is generally optimistic, you're better able to handle everyday stress more constructively. That ability may contribute to the widely observed health benefits of positive thinking.

Optimism is thinking positively about the things that will happen. A positive attitude, on the other hand, is about being positive in the way you think about things. Unlike optimism, a positive attitude doesn't invite falsehoods. It doesn't ask that you surrender your reasoning abilities to make decisions. Because a positive attitude aligns with the truth of your reality, you can be as positive as you like without the dangers of overconfidence or arrogance

However, even for accurate tools, there is still a huge range in the level of usefulness for each.

A Perspective Is Useful If It:

- Gives you more power
- Focuses you on the actionable part of the problem
- Makes you enthusiastic

Helen Keller's quote that I used earlier in the article is a great example. By saying life is either a daring adventure or nothing, she contrasts this useful attitude to the more common, defeatist perspective on life.

Positive thinking isn't about what you think, it's how you think. If you're optimistic about your results, you'll ultimately head away from reality and towards self-deception. If you're positive with your attitude, you make realistic decisions that inspire you to move forward.

Chapter:5

How to Recognize Negative Thought Patterns

Negative affectivity (NA), or negative affect, is a personality variable that involves the experience of negative emotions and poor self-concept. Negative affectivity subsumes a variety of negative emotions, including anger, contempt, disgust, guilt, fear, and nervousness. Low negative affectivity is characterized by frequent states of calmness and serenity, along with states of confidence, activeness, and great enthusiasm.

Individuals differ in negative emotional reactivity. Trait negative affectivity roughly corresponds to the dominant personality factor of anxiety/neuroticism that is found within the Big Five personality traits as emotional stability. The Big Five are characterized as openness, conscientiousness, extraversion, agreeableness, and neuroticism. Neuroticism can plague an individual with severe mood swings, frequent sadness, worry, and is easily disturbed, and predicts the development and onset of all "common" mental disorders. Research shows that negative affectivity relates to different classes of variables: Self-reported stress and (poor) coping skills, health complaints, and frequency of unpleasant events. Weight gain and mental health complaints are often experienced as well.

People who express high negative affectivity view themselves and a variety of aspects of the world around them in generally negative terms. Negative affectivity is strongly related to life satisfaction. Individuals high in negative affect will exhibit, on average, higher levels of distress, anxiety, and dissatisfaction, and tend to focus on the unpleasant aspects of themselves, the world, the future, and other people, and also evoke more negative life events. The similarities between these affective traits and life satisfaction have led some researchers to view both positive and negative affect with life satisfaction as specific indicators of the broader construct of subjective well-being.

Negative affect arousal mechanisms can induce negative affective states as evidenced by a study conducted by Stanley S. Seidner on negative arousal and white noise. The study quantified reactions from Mexican and Puerto Rican participants in response to the devaluation of speakers from other ethnic origins

Recent studies indicate that negative affect has important, beneficial impacts on cognition and behavior. These developments are a remarkable departure from past psychological research, which is characterized by a unilateral emphasis on the benefits of positive affect. Both states of affect influence mental processes and behavior. Negative affect is regularly recognized as a "stable, heritable trait tendency to experience a broad range of negative feelings, such as worry, anxiety, self-criticisms, and a negative self-view". This allows one to feel every type of emotion, which is regarded as a normal part of life and human nature. So, while the emotions themselves are viewed as negative, the individual experiencing them should not be classified as a negative person or depressed. They are going through a normal process and are feeling something that many individuals may not be able to feel or process due to differing problems.

These findings complement evolutionary psychology theories that affective states serve adaptive functions in promoting suitable cognitive strategies to deal with environmental challenges. Positive affect is associated with assimilative, top-down processing used in response to familiar, benign environments. Negative affect is connected with accommodative, bottom-up processing in response to unfamiliar, or problematic environments. Thus, positive affectivity promotes simplistic heuristic approaches that rely on preexisting knowledge and assumptions. Conversely, negative affectivity promotes controlled, analytic approaches that rely on externally drawn information.

Benefits of negative affect are present in areas of cognition including perception, judgment, memory and interpersonal personal relations. Since negative effect relies more on cautious processing than preexisting knowledge, people with negative affect tend to perform better in instances involving deception, manipulation, impression formation and stereotyping. Negative affectivity's analytical and detailed processing of information leads to fewer reconstructive-memory errors, whereas positive mood relies on the broader schematic to thematic information that ignores detail. Thus, information processing in negative moods reduces the misinformation effect and increases the overall accuracy of details. People also exhibit less interfering responses to stimuli when given descriptions or performing any cognitive task.

Judgment

People are notoriously susceptible to forming inaccurate judgments based on biases and limited information. Evolutionary theories propose that negative affective states tend to increase skepticism and decrease reliance on preexisting knowledge. Consequently, judgmental accuracy is improved in areas such as impression formation, reducing fundamental attribution error, stereotyping, and gullibility. While sadness is normally associated with the hippocampus, it does not produce the same side effects that would be associated with feelings of pleasure or excitement. Sadness correlates with feeling blue or the creation of tears, while excitement may cause a spike in blood pressure and one's pulse. As far as judgment goes, most people think about how they feel about a certain situation. They will jump right to their current mood when asked a question. However, some mistake this process when using their current mood to justify a reaction to a stimulus. If you're sad, yet only a little bit, chances are your reactions and input will be negative as a whole.

Impression Formation

First impressions are one of the most basic forms of judgments people make daily, yet judgment formation is a complex and fallible process. Negative affect is shown to decrease errors in forming impressions based on presuppositions. One common judgment error is the halo effect, or the tendency to form unfounded impressions of people based on known but irrelevant information. For instance, more attractive people are often attributed to more positive qualities. Research demonstrates that positive effect tends to increase the halo effect, whereas negative affect decreases it.

A study involving undergraduate students demonstrated a halo effect in identifying a middle-aged man as more likely to be a philosopher than an unconventional, young woman. These halo effects were nearly eliminated when participants were in a negative affective state. In the study, researchers sorted participants into either happy or sad groups using an autobiographical mood induction task in which participants reminisced on sad or happy memories. Then, participants read a philosophical essay by a fake academic who was identified as either a middle-aged, bespectacled man or as a young, unorthodox-looking woman. The fake writer was evaluated on intelligence and competence. The positive affect group exhibited a strong halo effect, rating the male writer significantly higher than the female writer's incompetence. The negative affect group exhibited almost no halo effects rating the two equally. Researchers concluded that impression formation is improved by negative affect. Their findings support theories that negative effect results in more elaborate processing based upon external, available information.

Fundamental Attribution Error

The systematic, attentive approach caused by negative affect reduces fundamental attribution error, the tendency to inaccurately attribute behavior to a person's internal character without taking external, situational factors into account. The fundamental attribution error (FAE) is connected with a positive effect since it occurs when people use top-down cognitive processing based on inferences. Negative affect stimulates bottom-up, systematic analysis that reduces fundamental attribution error.

This effect is documented in FAE research in which students evaluated a fake debater on attitude and likability based on an essay the "debater" wrote. After being sorted into positive or negative effect groups, participants read one of two possible essays arguing for one side or another on a highly controversial topic. Participants were informed that the debater was assigned a stance to take in the essay that did not necessarily reflect his views. Still, the positive affect groups rated debaters who argued unpopular views as holding the same attitude expressed in the essay. They were also rated as unlikeable compared to debaters with popular stances, thus, demonstrating FAE. In contrast, the data for the negative affect group displayed no significant difference in ratings for debaters with popular stances and debaters with unpopular stances. These results indicate that positive affect assimilation styles promote fundamental attribution error, and negative affect accommodation styles minimize the error in respect to judging people.

Stereotyping

Negative affect benefits judgment in diminishing the implicit use of stereotypes by promoting closer attention to stimuli. In one study, participants were less likely to discriminate against targets that appeared Muslim when in a negative affective state. After organizing participants into positive and negative affect groups, researchers had them play a computer game. Participants had to make rapid decisions to shoot only at targets carrying a gun. Some of the targets wore turbans making them appear Muslim. As expected, there was a significant bias against Muslim targets resulting in a tendency to shoot at them. However, this tendency decreased with subjects in negative affective states. Positive affect groups developed more aggressive tendencies toward Muslims. Researchers concluded that negative affect leads to less reliance on internal stereotypes, thus decreasing judgmental bias.

Gullibility

Multiple studies have shown that negative affectivity has a beneficial role in increasing skepticism and decreasing gullibility. Because negative affective states increase external analysis and attention to details, people in negative states are better able to detect deception.

Researchers have presented findings in which students in negative affective states had improved lie detection compared to students in positive affective states. In a study, students watched video clips of everyday people either lying or telling the truth. First, music was used to induce a positive, negative, or neutral effects in participants. Then, experimenters played 14 video messages that had to be identified by participants as true or false. As expected, the negative effect group performed better in veracity judgments than the positive affect group who performed no better than chance. Researchers believe that the negative effect groups detected deception more successfully because they attended to stimulus details and systematically built inferences from those details.

77

Memory

Memory has been found to have many failures that affect the accuracy of recalled memories. This has been especially pragmatic in criminal settings as eyewitness memories are less reliable than one would hope. However, the externally focused and accommodative processing of negative affect has a positive effect on the overall improvement of memory. This evidenced by the reduction of the misinformation effect and the number of false memories reported. The knowledge implies that negative affect can be used to enhance eyewitness memory; however, additional research suggests that the extent to which memory is improved by negative affect does not sufficiently improve eyewitness testimonies to significantly reduce its error.

Misinformation Effect

The negative effect has been shown to decrease the susceptibility of incorporating misleading information, which is related to the misinformation effect. The misinformation effect refers to the finding that misleading information presented between the encoding of an event and its subsequent recall influences a witness's memory. This corresponds to two types of memory failure:

Suggestibility: When recollections are influenced by the prodding or expectations of others creating false memories.

Misattribution: When a witness gets confused and misattributes the misinformation to the original event. Also defined as the retroactive interference: When later information interferes with the ability to retain previously encoded information.

In Witness of Events

Negative mood is shown to decrease suggestibility error. This is seen through reduced amounts of incorporation of false memories when misleading information is present. On the other hand, positive affect has shown to increase susceptibility to misleading information. An experiment with undergraduate students supported these results. Participants began the study in a lecture hall and witnessed what they thought was an unexpected five-minute belligerent encounter between an intruder and the lecturer. A week later, these participants watched a 10-minute-long video that generated either a positive, negative or neutral mood. They then completed a brief questionnaire about the previous incident between the intruder and lecturer that they witnessed the week earlier. In this questionnaire, half of the participants received questions with misleading information and the other half received questions without any misleading information. This manipulation was used to determine if participants were susceptible to suggestibility failure. After 45 minutes of unrelated distractors, participants were given a set of true or false questions that tested for false memories. Participants experiencing negative moods reported fewer numbers of false memories, whereas those experiencing positive moods reported a greater amount of false memories. This implies that a positive effect promotes the integration of misleading details and negative effect reduces the misinformation effect.

In Recall of Past Public Events

People who experience negative affectivity following an event report fewer reconstructive false memory. This was evidenced by two studies conducted around public events. The first surrounded the events of the televised O.J. Simpson trial. Participants were asked to fill out questionnaires three times: one week, two months and a year after the televised verdict. These questionnaires measured participant emotion towards the verdict and the accuracy of their recalled memory of what occurred during the trial. Overall, the study found that although participant response to the event outcome did not affect the quantity of remembered information, it did influence the likelihood of false memory. Participants who were pleased with the verdict of the O.J. Simpson trial were more likely to falsely believe something occurred during the trial than those who were displeased with the verdict. Another experiment found the same findings with Red Sox fans and Yankees fans in their overall memory of events that occurred in the final game of a 2004 playoff series in which the Red Sox defeated the Yankees. The study found that the Yankees fans had a better memory of events that occurred than the Red Sox fans. The results from both of these experiments are consistent with the findings that negative emotion can lead to fewer memory errors and thus increased memory accuracy of events.

Degree of Enhanced Memory

Although negative affect has been shown to decrease the misinformation effect, the degree to which memory is improved is not enough to make a significant effect on witness testimony. Emotions, including negative affect, are shown to reduce accuracy in identifying perpetrators from photographic lineups. Researchers demonstrated this effect in an experiment in which participants watched a video that induced either negative emotion or a neutral mood. The two videos were deliberately similar except for the action of interest, which was either a mugging (negative emotion) or a conversation (neutral emotion). After watching one of the two videos participants are shown perpetrator lineups, which either contained the target perpetrator from the video or a foil, a person that looked similar to the target. The results revealed that the participants who watched the emotion-induced video were more likely to incorrectly identify the innocent foil than to correctly identify the perpetrator. Neutral participants were more likely to correctly identify the perpetrator in comparison to their emotional counterparts. This demonstrates that emotional affect in forensic settings decreases the accuracy of eyewitness memory. These findings are consistent with prior knowledge that stress and emotion greatly impair eyewitness ability to recognition perpetrators.

Interpersonal Benefits

Negative affectivity can produce several interpersonal benefits. It can cause subjects to be more polite and considerate with others. Unlike positive mood, which causes less assertive approaches, negative affectivity can, in many ways, cause a person to be more polite and elaborate when making requests.

Negative affectivity increases the accuracy of social perceptions and inferences. Specifically, high negative-affectivity people have more negative, but accurate, perceptions of the impression they make to others. People with low negative affectivity form overly-positive, potentially inaccurate impressions of others that can lead to misplaced trust.

Intergroup Discrimination

A research conducted by Forgas J.P studied how affectivity can influence intergroup discrimination. He measured affectivity by how people allocate rewards to in-group and out-group members. In the procedure, participants had to describe their interpretations after looking at patterns of judgments about people. Afterward, participants were exposed to a mood induction process, where they had to watch videotapes designed to elicit negative or positive affectivity. Results showed that participants with positive affectivity were more negative and discriminated more than participants with negative affectivity. Also, happy participants were more likely to discriminate between in-group and out-group members than sad participants. Negative affect is often associated with team selection. It is viewed as a trait that could make selecting individuals for a team irrelevant, thus preventing knowledge from becoming known or predicted for current issues that may arise.

Communication

Negative affectivity subconsciously signals a challenging social environment. The negative mood may increase a tendency to conform to social norms.

In a study, college students were exposed to a mood induction process. After the mood induction process, participants were required to watch a show with positive and negative elements. After watching the show, they were asked to engage in a hypothetical conversation in which they "describe the episode (they) just observed to a friend". Their speech was recorded and transcribed during this task. Results showed that speakers in a negative mood had a better-quality description and a greater amount of information and details. These results show that a negative mood can improve people's communication skills.

A negative mood is closely linked to better conversation because it makes use of the hippocampus and different regions of the brain.[citation needed] When someone is upset, that individual may see or hear things differently than an individual who is very upbeat and happy all the time. The small details the negative individual picks up maybe something completely overlooked before. Anxiety disorders are often associated with over-thinking and ruminating on topics that would seem irrelevant and pointless to an individual without a disorder. OCD is one common anxiety trait that allows the affected individual a different insight into how things may appear to be. A person that makes use of his or her negative affect has a different view of the world and what goes on in it, thus making their conversations different and interesting to others.

Self-Disclosure

Results of one study show that participants with negative affectivity were more careful with the information they shared with others, being more cautious with who they could trust or not. Researchers found that negative mood not only decreases intimacy levels but also increases caution in placing trust in others.

Negative thinking is a thought process where people tend to find the worst in everything or reduce their expectations by considering the worst possible scenarios. This approach can allay disappointment in some situations; but negative thinking tends to manifest into a pattern that can cause tremendous stress, worry, or sadness over time. The opposite approach would be positive thinking, approaching situations or circumstances with a positive attitude.

Common Examples of Negative Thinking

I just won the lottery. The worst part is that I can't tell my family and friends because if I did, they'd all want some of the money.

A new higher paying job would be a good thing except for the change in the commute, possible reduction in health insurance and having to get to know a whole new group of people.

I can't imagine why anyone would want to live in a great big house with all that land. All I can think of is the heating bill, and cutting that grass!

I'd rather not own a highly successful restaurant. Sure, you could be famous and make a ton of money, but just think of those long hours and dealing with the public all the time.

You may say you want a cool sporty car, but I can't imagine paying that car insurance and getting pulled over by cops all the time.

It might be nice that I am graduating at the top of my class, but really, what difference does it make when I have to pay back all of these student loans?

Dogs could be great companions and brighten things up if they didn't make such a mess and all that noise.

My job pays well and fast tracks its employees into higher positions since they're growing so quickly, but sitting in a grey, boring cubicle listening to sad FM radio all afternoon from the cubicle next door is just too much.

Urban environments are great for restaurants and culture, but why would I live there if I am just going to constantly worried, I'm going to be assaulted or my house is going to be robbed?

Some people think all of this snow is pretty. I think it just ruins everything. You can't get to work, you have to shovel, and you can fall and hurt yourself. No thanks.

Having a king-size bed might sound nice, but it just takes up the whole room and the sheets are expensive.

Our trip to the Maldives would have been fabulous were it not for having to spend 14 hours in flight. No sleep, poor airline food, and noisy other passengers were no fun at all.

My husband cooked dinner tonight since I had a long day at work but it was only pasta - I mean, how hard is that?

I won a brand-new computer to replace my old broken one, but it has a whole new operating system that I have to learn now - who has time for that?

occasional anxiety is a normal part of life. You might worry about things like health, money, or family problems. But people with a generalized anxiety disorder (GAD) feel extremely worried or feel nervous about these and other things—even when it is little or no reason to worry about them. People with GAD find it difficult to control their anxiety and stay focused on daily tasks.

The good news is that GAD is treatable. Call your doctor to talk about your symptoms so that you can feel better.

What are the signs and symptoms of GAD?

GAD develops slowly. It often starts during the teen years or young adulthood. People with GAD may:

- Worry very much about everyday things

- Have trouble controlling their worries or feelings of nervousness
- Know that they worry much more than they should
- Feel restless and have trouble relaxing
- Have a hard time concentrating
- Be easily startled
- Have trouble falling asleep or staying asleep
- Feel easily tired or tired all the time
- Have headaches, muscle aches, stomach aches, or unexplained pains
- Have a hard time swallowing
- Tremble or twitch
- Be irritable or feel "on edge"
- Sweat a lot, feel light-headed or out of breath
- Have to go to the bathroom a lot
- Children and teens with GAD often worry excessively about:
- Their performance, such as in school or sports
- Catastrophes, such as earthquakes or war
- Adults with GAD are often highly nervous about everyday circumstances, such as:
- Job security or performance
- Health

- Finances
- The health and well-being of their children
- Being late
- Completing household chores and other responsibilities

Both children and adults with GAD may experience physical symptoms that make it hard to function and that interfere with daily life.

Symptoms may get better or worse at different times, and they are often worse during times of stress, such as with a physical illness, during exams at school, or during a family or relationship conflict.

What Causes GAD?

GAD sometimes runs in families, but no one knows for sure why some family members have it while others don't. Researchers have found that several parts of the brain, as well as biological processes, play a key role in fear and anxiety. By learning more about how the brain and body function in people with anxiety disorders, researchers may be able to create better treatments. Researchers are also looking for ways in which stress and environmental factors play a role.

How Is GAD Treated?

First, talk to your doctor about your symptoms. Your doctor should do an exam and ask you about your health history to make sure that an unrelated physical problem is not causing your symptoms. Your doctor may refer to you as a mental health specialist, such as a psychiatrist or psychologist.

GAD is generally treated with psychotherapy, medication, or both. Talk with your doctor about the best treatment for you.

Psychotherapy

A type of psychotherapy called cognitive-behavioral therapy (CBT) is especially useful for treating GAD. CBT teaches a person a different way of thinking, behaving, and reacting to situations that help him or her feel less anxious and worried. For more information on psychotherapy,

Medication

Doctors may also prescribe medication to help treat GAD. Your doctor will work with you to find the best medication and dose for you. Different types of medication can be effective in GAD:

- Selective serotonin reuptake inhibitors (SSRIs)
- Serotonin-norepinephrine reuptake inhibitors (SNRIs)
- Other serotonergic medication

Benzodiazepines

Doctors commonly use SSRIs and SNRIs to treat depression, but they are also helpful for the symptoms of GAD. They may take several weeks to start working. These medications may also cause side effects, such as headaches, nausea, or difficulty sleeping. These side effects are usually not severe for most people, especially if the dose starts low and is increased slowly over time. Talk to your doctor about any side effects that you have.

Buspirone is another serotonergic medication that can be helpful in GAD. Buspirone needs to be taken continuously for several weeks for it to be fully effective.

Benzodiazepines, which are sedative medications, can also be used to manage severe forms of GAD. These medications are powerfully effective in rapidly decreasing anxiety, but they can cause tolerance and dependence if you use them continuously. Therefore, your doctor will only prescribe them for brief periods if you need them.

Don't give up on treatment too quickly. Both psychotherapy and medication can take some time to work. A healthy lifestyle can also help combat anxiety. Make sure to get enough sleep and exercise, eat a healthy diet, and turn to family and friends who you trust for support.

For basic information about these and other mental health medications, visit http://www. nimh.nih.gov/health/topics/mental-health-medications. Visit the Food and Drug Administration's website (http://www.fda.gov/) for the latest information on warnings, patient medication guides, or newly approved medications.

What Is It Like to Have GAD?

"I was worried all the time and felt nervous. My family told me that there were no signs of problems, but I still felt upset. I dreaded going to work because I couldn't keep my mind focused. I was having trouble falling asleep at night and was irritated at my family all the time.

I saw my doctor and explained my constant worries. My doctor sent me to someone who knows about GAD. Now I am working with a counselor to cope better with my anxiety. I had to work hard, but I feel better. I'm glad I made that first call to my doctor."

How you think about the events and people in your life can either help you reframe things in more positive ways that help you cope or take you down a rabbit hole of negative thinking and feeling bad about yourself, other people, and your prospects. Unhealthy ways of thinking and reacting to things can cause depression and anxiety, prolong stressors, and create chronically stressed states of mind that can affect your heart health and immunity. You can't always control what you think, but you can learn to identify when you're sinking into a negative pattern, and then reboot and redirect your thinking along a more constructive or hopeful path. If you keep redirecting your negative thinking over months and years, you may even change the patterns of neural connections in your brain so that you react to life's events in more grounded ways, with less panic and judgment.

It's tricky to identify negative thinking patterns because our thoughts feel so immediate and true. We have a habit of accepting them uncritically, without questioning. Also, worrying about something bad that may happen can draw you in, making you feel like you're doing something about the problem, even when you're making things worse for yourself. For some of us, overthinking can feel like a proxy for control. By keeping thoughts of the stressor in mind, we may feel like we can control what's going to happen. Many of life's stressors are not controllable, so focusing too much on them just drains our mental and emotional energy and prolongs the body's stress response.

Following Are 3 Negative Thinking Patterns to Avoid—And What to Do Instead:

1. Negative Rumination

Although it's natural and can be healthy to self-reflect, reflection becomes problematic when it's negative, excessive, and repetitive. Rumination is a kind of negative thinking in which we get mentally stuck and keep spinning our wheels without making progress, like a car stuck in a snowdrift. Rumination can make you more and more anxious as you keep thinking of more and more negative outcomes that could happen. If you feel lonely, you may think about being lonely forever, never meeting the right partner, never having kids, losing all your friends, and ending up alone in a ditch. Ruminating can also make you feel depressed. You may focus on how bad you feel, why you feel so bad, what you did wrong to get in this situation, and how things could get worse and you could mess things up even more. Before you know it, you start to feel like a loser, and this interferes with your motivation to take steps to solve the problem.

What to Do Instead: Pay attention to when you're thinking starts to get repetitive or negative. When you notice rumination, make yourself break the cycle. Get up and do something else: Go for a walk or reach out to a friend (but don't continue the rumination out loud by whining to them). Don't overeat or drink too much alcohol to avoid negative thoughts. Try to change your thinking to a problem-solving focus that is more deliberate and strategic.

2. Overthinking

Overthinking is when you go over and over different choices in your mind, trying to imagine every possible outcome and everything that could happen in the future, to make sure you make a perfect choice. Your focus is on avoiding mistakes and risks. The problem with overthinking is that it's an attempt to control what isn't controllable. You don't have a magic eight-ball that can predict the future. With most choices, there are unknowns. For example, when you choose a partner in life, you don't know what situations the two of you will face and how your partner will react to each situation. Overthinking can take away your joy in situations like choosing a college, changing jobs, getting married, having kids, buying a house, and so on. It can make you too risk-averse and scared to act. It can keep you stuck, unable to leave a bad relationship or choose a different career path.

What to Do Instead: Limit the time you spend thinking about a decision before acting. Give yourself a deadline to decide, even if it feels uncomfortable. Only allow yourself to research a few alternative options — not everyone. Don't be so hard on yourself: You are only

human, and it's not the end of the world if you make a mistake. You can learn from it. Overthinking results from anxiety, so practice stress-
management techniques like yoga, running, nature walking, or meditating.

3. Cynical Hostility

Cynical hostility is a way of thinking and reacting that is characterized by angry mistrust of other people. You see other people as threats. They may cheat you, take advantage, let you down, deceive you, or otherwise cause you harm. Cynical hostility involves interpreting other people's behavior in the worst ways. You may think the driver ahead of you is being deliberately slow to frustrate you, or that a friend has an ulterior motive. Cynical hostility can ruin your relationships and increase your blood pressure. Research shows it is associated with heart disease and shorter telomeres, the protective coverings at the ends of your chromosomes that fray with age. (Shorter telomeres are a sign of cellular aging.)

What to Do Instead: Try to get some distance from your judging thoughts. Notice when you begin to think distrustfully, and deliberately think of alternative ways of seeing the situation. What are some more benevolent or less toxic motives for people's behavior? Learn to reserve judgment and look for the evidence before labeling people. Notice how your behavior may be pushing people away or prompting them to react negatively to you.

In India, when training elephants, handlers begin by chaining one of the elephant's legs to a tree. Over time, they gradually decrease the size of the chain until all it takes is a flimsy string to hold the elephant. It's not the string that restrains the massive animal. It's his mind.

Your mind limits you in the same way. It can mercilessly pick apart and criticize your every move while chewing on the "evidence" ceaselessly. It can second-guess and sabotage your relationships with insecurities and emotional walls. Your mind can keep you stuck and hold you back in all areas of your life, like the elephant's string.

But It Doesn't Have To.

By recognizing your negative thinking patterns, not buying into them, and turning them around, you can put your mind to work FOR YOU instead of against you.

Your Brain's Priority Is Your Survival Not Your Happiness

All humans tend to be more like Eeyore than Tigger.

Your brain is built to remember and focus more on bad experiences than positive ones. It was an evolutionary advantage that helped our ancestors survive by avoiding danger. This negativity bias is still active in your brain today and can get in the way of your happiness, up to your stress and worry levels, and damage your brain and health.

Each of us experiences the world uniquely because our brains add their subjective tint when giving meaning to incoming stimuli. The color your brain adds is determined by your physical brain function, memories, beliefs, and attitudes about yourself, others, and the world shaped by family, religion, school, and life experiences.

The material is largely negative because it's your brain's job to hold onto and learn from the bad to protect you in the future. This negative mental filter is typically below your conscious awareness, but it impacts how you respond to the world, act in relationships, and think of and talk to yourself. In other words, it creates your reality.

Your brain's priority is your survival, not your happiness.

Negative Thinking Gets Wired Into Your Brain

Over time, through the process of neuroplasticity, habitual negative thinking patterns become physical neural traits in your brain. If you get stressed out often about every little thing, your brain is going to forge and strengthen connections making it reactive and anxious. If you expect the worst in all situations, you're reinforcing this kind of thinking in your brain every time you engage in it.

The negative thought patterns in which you routinely engage become the default pathways for your neurons and the strings that tie you down and limit your life – just like the elephant. Eventually, you may find yourself trapped in a downward spiral of anxiety, stress, depression, which your brain is perpetuating in a continual feedback loop.

There's a traditional saying that the mind takes the shape it rests upon; the modern update is that the brain takes the shape the mind rests upon. For instance, if you regularly rest your mind upon worries, self-criticism, and anger, then your brain will gradually take that shape – will develop neural structures and dynamics of anxiety, low sense of worth, and prickly reactivity to others. On the other hand, if you regularly rest your mind upon, for example noticing you're all right now, seeing the good in yourself and letting go…then your brain will gradually take the shape of calm strength, self-confidence, and inner peace."

The Most Common Negative Thinking Traps

Some of the most common negative thinking patterns, which you may recognize and indulge in are:

Black and white thinking: "I' can't even do this. I never do anything right."

Mind reading: "They think I'm boring. I know they have better things to do than hang out with me."

Crystal-ball gazing: "There's no point in even trying. I know I'm not going to get the job anyway."

Over-generalization: "This relationship didn't work out. I'm never going to meet someone."

Disqualifying the positive: "I may be a decent mother, but anybody can do that."

Over-reacting: "My friend hasn't replied to my text in 3 hours. She hates me. Nobody likes me."

Unrealistic expectations: "I have to get straight As. Nothing less is good enough."

Name-calling: "I can't believe I said that. I'm such an idiot."

Self-blame: "The boss looks mad. It must be something I did wrong."

Catastrophizing: "Since I can't pay this bill, my credit rating will go down the tubes and I'll lose the house."

How to Reverse Negative Thinking Patterns

Become Aware of Habitual Negative Thought Patterns

The first step in reversing negative thinking patterns is to become aware of them. You have to "catch" yourself in the act. You may be surprised and saddened by how often you engage in some of the types of thinking listed above. One way to do to become aware of your thoughts, feelings, and reactions as they happen, is mindfulness.

You can't control the random thoughts that pop into your mind. However, you can become aware of them, pause, and choose what happens next.

Challenge Your Thinking

Distance yourself from and question your thoughts and beliefs. Analyze them objectively from all angles. Is this really what you think or is it an inherited belief from your past? Drop the storylines usually running in your head and any personal emotional investment you have in the situation for a minute. Try on different points of view and zoom out. Have the intent to give your mind guidance, like a wise, caring friend. Control it instead of it controlling you.

Is Thought Helping or Hurting?

As a continuation of the step above, I like to ask myself "Is this thought helping me or hurting me?"

Usually, the answer is "It's hurting". When it is, I then consciously choose a thought that is more supportive, understanding, or positive. It's just as easy to come up with thoughts that encourage and help you achieve your goals as ones that don't help you. You have to become aware of your thoughts, pause, and make the effort to shift your thinking.

Your brain secretes neurochemicals and physically reacts to the thoughts that run through your mind. If you are guilty of frequently telling yourself things like "They don't like me" or "That was stupid", how do you think that kind of thinking makes you feel? Studies show that positive self-reflection, recalling happy memories, and affirmative thoughts boost serotonin activity in your prefrontal cortex.

After examining your thoughts mindfully, consciously decide what you want to believe and think, how you want to behave, and who you want to be. Hold that image at the forefront of your mind and move forward taking the appropriate actions. Deciding isn't a one-time thing. The priorities upon which you decide have to be considered and honored in the little choices you make every day and revisited as things change and new information becomes available.

For further guidance, here are 5 Ways to Work With Your Mind to Stop Negative Thoughts.

I was depressed for decades and tried to commit suicide which resulted in a serious brain injury. I had to learn the basics of living, thinking, and being again. This time around, I learned healthier, happier, kinder ways of thinking. By consciously working with and altering my thoughts, behaviors, and emotions, I transformed my world which in turn, changed my physical brain and its default mode of operation.

Today, I live a brain-healthy lifestyle incorporating mental health practices daily to maintain the balance and happiness I've found. I've made friends with my mind and have even learned to put it to work FOR me instead of AGAINST me. The difference in my life has been amazing. I like it much better this way

Negative thinking is something we all engage in from time to time, but constant negativity can destroy your mental health, leaving you depressed and anxious.

Science shows that positive thinking can improve mental wellbeing, minimize stress and even lead to better cardiovascular health, yet many of us are stuck following patterns of negative thinking. Let's explore the effects of negativity on mental health while looking at ways to end the cycle.

What Counts as Negative Thinking?

If you're someone who analyzes your thoughts, it can be challenging to differentiate negative thinking from the regular worries that everyone has. Feeling sad about an upsetting event is normal, just as worrying about financial burdens or relationship troubles is something, we all do from time to time. It's when those feelings are repetitive and pervasive, however, that problems arise

The negative thinking definition from Rethink Mental Illness stipulates that:

"Negative thinking refers to a pattern of thinking negatively about yourself and your surroundings. While everyone experiences negative thoughts now and again, negative thinking that seriously affects the way you think about yourself and the world and even interferes with work/study and everyday functioning could be a symptom of mental illness, including depression, anxiety disorders, personality disorders, and schizophrenia."

Not everyone who engages in negative thinking has a mental illness, just like not everyone with a mental illness has constant negative thoughts. However, negative thinking can be detrimental to your mental health and quality of life, particularly when you can't stop. Luckily, there are ways to end negative thoughts, but you must first look at what causes them.

What Are the Causes of Negative Thinking?

Negative thinking has many different causes. Intrusive negative thoughts can be a symptom of obsessive-compulsive disorder (OCD), generalized anxiety disorder (GAD) or another mental health condition. Negative thinking is also symptomatic of depression ("Negative Thinking and Depression: How One Fuels the Other"). While negative thinking can be a sign of mental ill-health, it can also be a regular part of life. Negative thoughts can impact your life severely, however, so it's best to get to the bottom of them, whatever the cause.

According to the Power of Positivity, there are three leading causes of negative thoughts.

Fear of the future: People often fear the unknown and are unsure what the future might bring. This often leads to "catastrophizing," which means always predicting failure and disaster. Whichever way you look at it, worrying about the future is a waste of time and energy. The key to letting go of these negative thoughts is to accept there is a limit to what you can change in the future and strive to focus on the present instead.

Anxiety about the present: Anxiety about the present is understandable. Many of us worry about what people think of us, whether we're doing a good job at work and what the traffic will be like on the way home. Negative thinkers often come up with the worst-case scenario: that no one in the office likes us, our boss is about to tell us we've done terrible work, and the traffic will make us late to pick up the kids. Again, this derives from the fear of losing control. Organization and routine can help with banishing negative thoughts, but you may also need to try practical therapy techniques.

Shame about the past: Have you ever lain awake worrying about something you did last week, or even last year? Everyone does and says things they feel embarrassed about, but negative thinkers tend to dwell on past mistakes and failures more than others. Of course, a more constructive way to approach mistakes is to accept that the event happened and consider how you could prevent it from happening again in the future.

How to Stop Negative Thinking Once and For All?

You don't have to succumb to a life of negative thinking. With some basic countering techniques, you can learn to get rid of negative thoughts by intercepting them before they become all-consuming. The key is to practice countering exercises every time you have a negative thought, and not to give up if you have a blip.

With this in mind, here are five questions to ask yourself next time negative thoughts arise. You can do this exercise in your head or by writing down your answers in a journal.

Is the thought true? Is there a basis for this negative belief?

Is the thought of giving you power, or is it taking your power away?

Can you put a positive spin on this thought or learn from it?

What would your life look like if you didn't have these negative beliefs?

Is the thought glossing over an issue that needs addressing?

Remember that countering negative thoughts takes time and commitment. Often, people require ongoing help from a mental health professional to change their negative thinking patterns for good ("How to Create Positivity in Life When You Have a Mental Illness").

laming myself -- While it's important to take responsibility for your part, excessive self-blame isn't productive. It's been linked to mental health problems, like depression. Be on the lookout for times when you tell yourself that you've "ruined everything" or that something is "all your fault."

Looking for bad news -- If nine good things and one bad thing happen in a day, it's easy to focus on the one bad part. But dwelling on the negative will keep you stuck in a dark place. It's important to step back and create a more balanced, realistic outlook.

Unhappy guessing -- Even though you have no idea what will happen tomorrow, you might predict doom and gloom. Whether you imagine that you're going to embarrass yourself in a meeting or tell yourself that you'll never get a promotion, unhappy guessing can turn into a self-fulfilling prophecy if you're not careful.

Exaggeratedly negative -- Telling yourself that the entire interview was a complete disaster or convincing yourself that everything about your job is terrible leads to a downward spiral. The more negatively you think, the worse you'll feel. And the worse you feel, the less likely you are to take positive action.

Chapter:6

How to Slow Down Thought Momentum

The transformed, evolved, or new, state of consciousness is to move through life in a simple state of "pure awareness" without needing to interpret and label everything through the "conditioning" of the mind. Let the "awareness" talk, let the "awareness" work, let the "awareness" write, and listen, and watch.

The transformed, evolved, or new, state of consciousness is to move through life in a simple state of "pure awareness" without needing to interpret and label everything through the "conditioning" of the mind. Let the "awareness" talk, let the "awareness" work, let the "awareness" write, and listen, and watch.

Moving through the conditioned mind is like watching life through tinted glasses. You will never have a clear vision. You don't need these glasses, so just let go of them and come to pure vision. The unconditioned intelligence of pure awareness can transform your entire reality and it does so without creating any conflict in the totality.

Your mind will automatically start resting more and more, as it allows the intelligence of "pure awareness" to take over from it. You will notice that the pace of your noisy thoughts is slowing down and a silent intelligence is working in your life.

The learning theory suggests that positive thinking can be learned. An athlete trains for several weeks or months an external behavior. He carries a certain behavior, and after some time he masters it. Thoughts can be understood as the internal behavior of a person. When we consciously practice some time a positive mental behavior, then our mind accustoms to positive thinking. It automatically responds to certain external situations with positive thoughts.

Positive thoughts lead to positive feelings. And positive feelings lead to health and happiness. To train positive thoughts has a great gain. It gives us a happy and healthy life. Especially if we practice also regularly sports (yoga, walking), enough relaxation (enough breaks, enough sleep, daily meditating) and a healthy diet (at least an apple a day).

How to learn positive thoughts? The learning method consists of four steps. First, we need a positive thought system that suits us like the philosophy of happiness. The philosophy of happiness teaches us to make happy to the center of life. The essence of the philosophy of happiness is the five qualities of wisdom, peace, love, strength, and joy. These five properties we practice every day.

The second step is systematically to train positive thoughts. The best way is to remember every morning on the five positive qualities. We create a positive plan of the day. We get up with a positive thought. We retain our positive vision during the day. And at night we think about the day and what we can do better the next day. We feel our negative emotions (fear, anger, grief, addiction). What negative thought is associated with it?

What positive thought helps us to overcome it? Which thought brings us into a positive attitude towards life? Helpful positive phrases are, "I'm a winner. I reach my goals. Wisdom is to organize my life so that I can live healthy and happy. "

The third step is to observe consistently our thoughts throughout the day and to stop all negative thoughts. If we recognize a negative thought, we push him away immediately. We consider what positive thought is helpful right now. We develop a positive thought and set it in place of the negative thought. If we make this in the long term, our negative thoughts are becoming less and our positive thoughts grow more and more. Nils was able to overcome his depression with this technique.

The constant observation of thought is the essence of positive thinking. Often, we overcome our negative thoughts already through the constant observation of our minds. We are aware of our negative thoughts and that already deprives them of their power. Sometimes we have to intervene forcefully. And just at the beginning of our mental work, we should be relatively strict with our thoughts. If our inner children are educated well, we can give them a little more freedom.

The fourth step is the stabilization of positive thinking. It is not easy all day to control our negative thoughts. We need strong helpers to keep us on our long-term path of inner happiness. Such helpers are the daily spiritual reading in a book, the daily oracle reading, the daily meditation, walking and a group of positive thinking people. Very good it is to distribute some caregivers throughout the day. We create a system of daily happiness exercises. We're putting so many exercises for us in the right intervals in the day that we keep ourselves constantly on the path of the positive. We stay with perseverance on our way of wisdom and happiness. If we fall off the path once, we stand up again the next day. In particularly difficult situations helps the constant change of lying (hearing meditation music), reading (praying, chanting), sports (yoga, walking) and work (doing good to others). We are practicing it for so long until our negative emotions have calmed down and we are positive again.

What Feelings in You Right Now?

The supreme principle of conduct in suffering situations is outwardly behaving properly and at the same time managing the thoughts and feelings as well as possible. Is the difficult situation outside gone, we can heal our emotional wounds? At certain points of the problem, we got inner tensions. This tension must be resolved again when the external stress situation is over. When we don´t heal our self after stressful situations, they remain permanently in our mind. In the long term, they affect our mental well-being. They lead to neurotic behavior and can cause physical illnesses.

If a problem affects you emotionally, it is good to do a helpful ritual. Think first about the problem. Thinking leads to constructive engagement with the problem. You realize that you can do something. You are not a helpless victim. You can live as a winner. You can solve the problem in any way. What is your helpful idea about your problem? "My idea is …"

Read a few pages in a spiritual book. Think about which book you need now. A spiritual book has a positive energy field. If we spend some time in this energy field, we get a positive spirit. Which book will strengthen your positive energy? Read it! After reading, take a walk for an hour or dance for 20 minutes as you like. Move all the rage and excitement out of your body. Think a Mantra (a positive sentence) and do a meditation (stop your thinking five minutes). Then think about your problem. Usually, you will come to rest mentally in half an hour. Half an hour then go just you like. Then you'll see things. You will be able to have positive ideas. Make after the walk some yoga exercises (creative hatha yoga) and long meditation in sitting (meditation with the inner voice) or lying down. Hook up a nice music and remain to lie down for so long, until your mind completely is at rest. Arise then again, eat something nice and think about what you need now. Give it yourself. Often it is very helpful to do something creative. We can paint, write, make music and express our feelings in our way. We can do something good for our fellow human beings and thus bring us into the energy of love. What is your way of love now?

If the problem is very big, you can do several rounds of reading, walking, doing good, enjoying and meditating. Usually, you get then to the point, where peace arises within you. Be very gentle with you and heal emotionally more and more. If a problem cannot be solved in one day, stop after a while you're thinking about the problem. Forbid you every further reflection. Avoid harmful rumination, which leads to nothing and only reinforces the internal stress. For large problems, you can take every day a certain time for problem handling.

To solve emotional problems is a creative process. You must feel exactly what you need now. What is currently the best way to solve your problem, to find inner peace and positivity? People are different and require different strategies. It is important to avoid self-defeating behaviors, such as tablets, smoke, drink, drugs, alcohol or eating too many sweets. It is better to manage the problem with the techniques of inner happiness. Then we grow spiritually on our problems. We grow inwardly on the problems of life until we will find everlasting happiness.

Happy in Five Minutes

In every life, there is pain, loss, illness, loneliness, and death. We have no claim to a long life still to be spared by fate. What is your pain today?

1. The problem: Describe briefly your situation and your problem. How exactly is your situation? What is the problem? Where is the center of the problem?

2. The Emotions: What are the feelings it in you? Fear, anger, addiction/desire, grief. What feeling is strongest? Where is the feeling sitting in your body?

3. The thoughts: What thoughts are connected with your feelings? Why are you sad, anxious, angry or longing? Count all your stressful thoughts down. (My thoughts are ...)

4. Thinking: What triggers your problem? What is the way out of your problem? What brings you to love, success, fulfillment, satisfaction? Think about your problem for so long, until you find a solution. Think about different solutions. Collect all the information you need.

5. Implementation: Follow your positive thoughts. Fulfill your positive life plan. Avoid meaningless brooding. Now is the time to realize powerful. Go your way to victory. "My positive sentence is ...."

Chapter:7

Why Nighttime Is the Worst Time for Overthinking

Those with nightmares experience abnormal sleep architecture and that the results of having a nightmare during the night were very similar to those of people who have insomnia. This is thought to be caused by frequent nocturnal awakenings and fear of falling asleep.

Classification

According to the International Classification of Sleep Disorders-Third Edition the nightmare disorder, together with REM sleep behavior disorder (RBD) and recurrent isolated sleep paralysis form the REM-related parasomnias subcategory of the Parasomnias cluster. Nightmares may be idiopathic without any signs of psychopathology or associated with disorders like stress, anxiety, substance abuse, psychiatric illness or PTSD patients report nightmares).] As regarding the dream content of the dreams they are usually imprinting negative emotions like sadness, fear or rage. According to the clinical studies the content can range from being chased, injury or death of others, falling, natural disasters or accidents. Typical dreams or recurrent dreams may also have some of these topics.

Cause

Scientific research shows that nightmares may have many causes. In a study focusing on children, researchers were able to conclude that nightmares directly correlate with the stress in children's lives. Children who experienced the death of a family member or a close friend or know someone with a chronic illness have more frequent nightmares than those who are only faced with stress from school or stress from social aspects of daily life. A study researching the causes of nightmares focuses on patients who have sleep apnea. The study was conducted to determine whether or not nightmares may be caused by sleep apnea, or being unable to breathe. In the nineteenth century, authors believed that nightmares were caused by not having enough oxygen, therefore it was believed that those with sleep apnea had more frequent nightmares than those without it. The results showed that healthy people have more nightmares than sleep apnea patients. Another study supports the hypothesis. In this study, 48 patients (aged 20–85 yrs) with obstructive airway disease (OAD), including 21 with and 27 without asthma, were compared with 149 sex- and age-matched controls without respiratory disease. OAD subjects with asthma reported approximately 3 times as many nightmares as controls or OAD subjects without asthma. The evolutionary purpose of nightmares then could be a mechanism to awaken a person who is in danger.

Lucid-dreaming advocate Stephen LaBerge has outlined a possible reason for how dreams are formulated and why nightmares occur with a high frequency. To LaBerge, a dream starts with an individual thought or scene, such as walking down a dimly lit street. Since dreams are not predetermined, the brain responds to the situation by either thinking a good thought or a bad thought, and the dream framework follows from there. Since the prominence of bad thoughts in dreams is higher than good,[further explanation needed] the dream will proceed to be a nightmare.

There is a view, possibly featured in the story A Christmas Carol, that eating cheese before sleep can cause nightmares, but there is little scientific evidence for this phenomenon.

Treatment

Sigmund Freud and Carl Jung seemed to have shared a belief that people frequently distressed by nightmares could be re-experiencing some stressful events from the past.[15] Both perspectives on dreams suggest that therapy can provide relief from the dilemma of the nightmarish experience.

Halliday (1987), grouped treatment techniques into four classes. Direct nightmare interventions that combine compatible techniques from one or more of these classes may enhance overall treatment effectiveness

Analytic and cathartic techniques

Storyline alteration procedures

Face-and-conquer approaches

Desensitization and related behavioral techniques.

Posttraumatic Stress Disorder

Recurring post-traumatic stress disorder nightmares in which traumas are re-experienced respond well to a technique called imagery rehearsal. This involves dreamers coming up with alternative, mastery outcomes to the nightmares, mentally rehearsing those outcomes while awake, and then reminding themselves at bedtime that they wish these alternate outcomes should the nightmares reoccur. Research has found that this technique not only reduces the occurrence of nightmares and insomnia but also improves other daytime PTSD symptoms. The most common variations of Imagery Rehearsal Therapy (IRT) "relate to the number of sessions, duration of treatment, and the degree to which exposure therapy is included in the protocol". The medication prazosin appears useful in decreasing the number of nightmares and the distress caused by them in people with PTSD.

Epidemiology

Fearfulness in waking life is correlated with nightmares.[21] Studies of dreams have estimated that about 75% of the time, the emotions evoked by dreams are negative.[21] However, it is worth noting that people are more likely to remember unpleasant dreams.

One definition of "nightmare" is a dream which causes one to wake up in the middle of the sleep cycle and experience a negative emotion, such as fear. This type of event occurs on average once per month. They are not common in children under five, but they are more common in young children (25% experiencing a nightmare at least once per week), most common in teenagers, and common in adults (dropping in frequency about one third from age 25 to 55) The prevalence in children

Nightmare disorder, also known as dream anxiety disorder, is a sleep disorder characterized by frequent nightmares. The nightmares, which often portray the individual in a situation that jeopardizes their life or personal safety, usually occur during the REM stages of sleep. Though most people have experienced at least one nightmare during their life, subjects with nightmare disorder experience them with a greater frequency. The disorder's DSM-IV number is 307.47.

Nightmare disorders are included in the parasomnias, which cover all the unusual behaviors during sleep. Nightmare disorders can be confused with sleep terror disorders. The difference is that after a sleep terror episode, the patient wakes up with more dramatic symptoms than for a nightmare disorder, such as screaming and crying. Furthermore, they don't remember the reason for the fear, while a patient with a nightmare disorder remembers every detail of the dream. Finally, sleep terrors usually occur during NREM Sleep.

Nightmares also have to be distinguished from bad dreams, which are less emotionally intense. Furthermore, nightmares contain more stories of aggression than bad dreams and more unhappy endings. Finally, people experiencing nightmares feel more fear than for bad dreams.

Signs and Symptoms

A Boy Having A Nightmare

During the nightmare, the sleeper may scream and yell out things. The nightmare sufferer is often awakened by these threatening, frightening dreams and can often vividly remember their experience. Upon awakening, the sleeper is usually alert and oriented within their surroundings, but may have an increased heart rate and symptoms of anxiety, like sweating. They may have trouble falling back to sleep for fear they will experience another nightmare.

A person experiencing nightmare disorder may have trouble going through everyday tasks; anxiety and lack of sleep caused by the fearful dreams may hinder the individual from completing everyday jobs efficiently and correctly. Upon experiencing this, these nightmare sufferers may consult with a psychiatrist.

The sleeper may have recurring episodes of awakening while recalling the intensely disturbing dream manifestations which usually result from fear or anxiety, but can also be triggered from anger, sadness, disgust, and other dysphoric emotions. The sleeper also can endure at least one of the following two features: delayed return of going back to sleep after episodes, and having episodes in the latter half of the patient's sleep.

Consequences

Nightmare disorder is common: it affects about 4% of the adult population. Even if children have more nightmares than adults, only 1% of children meet the criteria of the disorder. Nightmare disorder can impair the quality of life for the people who are affected by the condition. It can make the patient avoid sleep, which leads to sleep deprivation which could lead to even more intense nightmares for the patient. Some other consequences of nightmare disorder are fatigue and insomnia.

Nightmare disorders have negative consequences in several fields, such as sleep, cognitive and emotional functioning, and well-being. Nightmares can also hurt the bed partner's life.

Content of Idiopathic Nightmares

Physical aggression is the main theme of nightmares. Other fields, such as interpersonal conflict, failure, helplessness, apprehension, being chased, accident, an evil force, disaster, insects and environmental abnormality could also be part of nightmares. Fear is the most frequent emotion associated with these nightmares, even if other emotions such as sadness, anger, and confusion can also be present.

Criteria

According to the International Classification of Sleep Disorders, the criteria needed to diagnose a nightmare disorder are the following. First, the presence of frequent nightmares that imply a danger for the person and that impact mood negatively is needed. Second, when waking up from nightmares, the person behaves in an alert way. Finally, the disorder has to impact clinically in a significant way the personal, social or professional functioning, in areas such as mood, sleep, cognition, behavior, fatigue, family, and occupation.

Causes

Nightmares can be caused by
extreme pressure or irritation if no other mental disorder is discovered. The death of a loved one or a stressful life event can be enough to cause a nightmare but mental conditions such as post-traumatic stress disorder and other psychiatric disorders have been known to cause nightmares as well. If the individual is on medication, the nightmares may be attributed to some side effects of the
drug. Amphetamines, antidepressants,
and stimulants like cocaine and caffeine can cause nightmares. Blood pressure medication, levodopa, and medications for Parkinson's disease have also been known to cause nightmares.

The nightmares may be idiopathic or could be associated with psychiatric disorders like post-traumatic stress disorder, schizophrenia, and borderline personality disorder. Nightmares can also be triggered by stress and anxiety and substance abuse, such as drugs that affect the neurotransmitters norepinephrine and dopamine and se rotonin. Nevertheless, causality between drugs such as beta-blockers or alpha-agonists and nightmares is still unclear and further researches need to be done to investigate the biochemical mechanisms of nightmares.

Eighty percent of patients who suffer from PTSD report nightmares. Patients suffering from PTSD have symptoms that are classified into three clusters: intrusive/re-experiencing, numbing, and hyperarousal. Nightmares are usually considered to be part of the intrusive/re-experiencing symptom.

Some differences are existing between idiopathic and PTSD related nightmares. A PTSD person having nightmares would wake up during the night more frequently and for a longer time than with idiopathic nightmares. Consequently, people with PTSD would have poorer sleep quality. Furthermore, nightmares related to PTSD would be more stressful than idiopathic ones. However, further studies have to be conducted in this area to obtain more reliable results.

Assessment

Polysomnography records physiological parameters, such as electroencephalography (EEG), electromyography (EMG) and electrooculography (EOG) in a sleep laboratory. However, the frequency of posttraumatic nightmares tends to decrease in an artificial lab setting, which would impact the content of nightmares. Consequently, assessment of nightmare disorders using polysomnography has to last for a longer period, to let the patient getting used to the arterial environment.

Self-report by a questionnaire or by a diary is another way to investigate nightmare disorders. However, these methods are questionable. Indeed, when filling out questionnaires with questions about a long period, people often tend to underestimate the frequency of their nightmares because of forgetting. On the contrary, filling out a diary every day may lead to an overestimation of the numbers of nightmares, because of the focus on this phenomenon.

Comorbidity

Studies have reported that nightmare disorders were present in 50- 70% of the cases for PTSD, 17.5% for depression, 18.3% for insomnia, 16.7% for schizophrenia and 49% for borderline personality disorders. For all psychiatric disorders taken together, nightmare disorders are present in 29.9% of the cases, a much bigger rate than for the general population, which is 2-5%. Nightmare disorders can also be associated with sleep disorders such as night terrors, chronic insomnia and sleep-disordered breathing. The presence of nightmares before a trauma would influence the severity of PTSD symptoms. Furthermore, having nightmares is linked to a significantly higher risk of attempting suicide and death by suicide.

Nightmares also seem to be correlated with some personality factors. Studies found an association between anxiety, depression, and nightmares in insomnia, while the only small relationship was found in other populations. Neuroticism would be also linked to nightmares. Nevertheless, people with a higher score of neuroticisms could be better at recalling their nightmares during the self-report assessment, which could influence this association.

Treatment

Stress reduction techniques such as yoga, meditation and exercise may help to eliminate stress and create a more peaceful sleeping atmosphere.

Diagnosis and medication can only be given to patients that report the recurring nightmares to a psychiatrist or other physician. Medications like prazosin are sometimes used to treat nightmares in people with PTSD. Therapy usually helps to deal with the frightening themes of the nightmares and alleviate the recurrence of the dreams. The persistent nightmares will usually improve as the patient gets older. Therapy is usually efficient to treat chronic nightmares in PTSD disorder or other populations. Medication has shown efficacy to treat chronic nightmares among a PTSD population but the impact of pharmacological treatments on other populations, such as drug-related nightmares, is unknown. Furthermore, patients usually take more than one medication at a time, whatever the cause related to nightmares, leading to possible interactive effects.

Eye Movement Desensitization and Reprocessing (EMDR) has demonstrated a significant nightmares' reduction, especially for the treatment of PTSD. Silver, Brooks, and Obenchain have found a decrease in the nightmares with Vietnam War veterans after 90 days of EMDR. Jayatunge has found significant results with people who have survived a tsunami. Greenwald has successfully used EMDR with children. There wasn't any negative consequence due to the EMDR sessions.

Research has been undertaken to investigate if sufferers of nightmares could benefit from the ability to be aware that they are indeed dreaming, a process known as lucid dreaming. Lucid Dreaming Therapy is a specific method of Imagery Rehearsal Therapy. The dreamer is conscious during his dream and can modulate it. Consequently, anxiety decreases, controllability increases, expectations change, which will impact the frequency of nightmares. Several studies have shown significant results with the lucid dreaming therapy. Two studies indicate a decrease of the nightmare frequency after only 12 weeks and one study shows, in 80% of the cases, the total disappearance of the nightmares after one year. Although these studies showed the efficacy of this therapy in the reduction of nightmare frequency on patients from the general population, so far evidence for this treatment is still weak.

Imagery Rehearsal Therapy has been shown as efficient to treat nightmare disorder in PTSD as well as in non-PTSD populations. In this treatment, the person has to write a new scenario of the nightmare with positive images that will be rehearsed for 10 to 20 minutes per day, to change the negative content of the nightmare. Cognitive Behavioral Therapy for Insomnia is also efficient to treat nightmares in the PTSD population. This method aims to change sleep habits with a clinician's help and the use of tools such as a sleep diary.

Exposure, relaxation and restriping therapy are used to treat PTSD related nightmares. This intervention combines Imagery Rehearsal Therapy with exposure and relaxation techniques. The main objective is to work on the trauma-related themes of nightmares.

Systematic Desensitization, using graduated exposure, is efficient to treat chronic nightmares. The person has to face the frightening elements of nightmares gradually, from the less to the most stressful. When a person starts to feel insecure, she has to manage the stress by applying a relaxation technique.

Pharmacological Treatments

Pharmacological treatments could be also efficient to treat nightmare disorder. Most of the treatments were assessed to patients suffering from PTSD. The most efficient is an alpha-blocker, named Prazosin, which reduces tone during sleep by blocking noradrenergic receptors. Prazosin would significantly decrease the number of PTSD related nightmares and would, therefore, improve sleep quality. However, only a few studies considered the effect of Prazosin in idiopathic nightmares. Benzodiazepines are also often used to treat nightmare disorder, despite the lack of efficacy demonstrated in empirical studies. Some patients were also treated with atypical antipsychotic medications. Olanzapine has quickly decreased nightmares. Two studies have shown the positive effects of Risperidone. Aripiprazole is more tolerated than olanzapine and has demonstrated substantial improvement in the nightmare frequency. Some other drugs as clonidine, cyproheptadine, fluvoxamine, gabapentin, nabilone, phenelzine, topiramate or trazodone have presented an amelioration of the nightmares. But some further researches are needed.

Epidemiology

About 4% of American adults are affected by nightmare disorders. Women seem to be more affected than men, the ratio being 2-4: 1. This inequality decreases with aging because of less high prevalence in elderly women. However, it is still unclear if the difference in prevalence between men and women is real or if it reflects a higher dream recall capacity of women.

According to studies, children at the age of 6–10 years are 41% more likely to experience nightmares and 22% at the age of 11.[32] Children with persistent nightmares range from 10% to 50%. However, only 1% of children meet the criteria of a nightmare disorder. Some factors tend to predict the development of a disorder from the presence of nightmares during childhood, such as a fear of going to sleep or going back to bed after a nightmare, an irregular sleep life and an avoidance of thinking about the nightmare.

Research

Dissociative disorders are usually paired with Nightmare Disorder 57% of the time. Nightmare disorder is believed to be associated with Dissociative Disorders as a defense mechanism that is used to escape from the traumatic event that caused the Dissociative Disorder. People with Dissociative Disorder and Nightmare disorder are more likely to self-mutilate, attempt suicide, and have Borderline Personality Disorder.

Borderline personality disorder with Nightmare Disorder is very common since the stages of sleep vary from that of a normal person (i.e. increased stage one sleep, and less stage four sleep). People with Borderline Personality disorder and Nightmare Disorder are usually the severest of those who have Borderline Personality Disorder; therefore, treating those with Nightmares Disorder may also help some with Borderline Personality Disorder.

Hypnosis seems to be a new and effective treatment for those with Nightmare Disorder since it increases relaxation.

Nightmare disorder is also associated with those who have lower cholesterol. This connection is unclear; however, cholesterol may affect other hormones in the body (such as serotonin) which may affect one's sleep

From the 1881 Household Cyclopedia. its bad Great attention is to be paid to regularity and choice of diet. Intemperance of every kind is hurtful, but nothing is more productive of this disease than drinking bad wine. Of eatables, those which are most prejudicial are all fat and greasy meats and pastry. These are needed to be avoided, or eaten with caution. The same may be said of salt meats, for which dyspeptic patients have frequently a remarkable predilection, but which are not on that account the less unsuitable.

Moderate exercise contributes to a superior degree to promote the digestion of food and prevent flatulence; those, however, who are necessarily confined to a sedentary occupation, should particularly avoid applying themselves to study or bodily labor immediately after eating. If a strong propensity to sleep should occur after dinner, it will be certainly better to indulge in a little, as the process of digestion frequently goes on much better during sleep than when awake.

Going to bed before the usual hour is a frequent cause of night-mare, as it either occasions the patient to sleep too long or to lie long awake in the night. Passing a whole night or part of a night without rest likewise gives birth to the disease, as it occasions the patient, on a succeeding night, to sleep too soundly. Indulging in sleep too late in the morning is an almost certain method to bring on the paroxysm, and the more frequently it returns, the greater strength it acquires; the propensity to sleep at this time is almost irresistible. Those who are habitually subject to attacks of the night-mare ought never to sleep alone but should have some person near them, to be immediately awakened by their groans and struggles, and the person to whom this office may be entrusted should be instructed to rouse the patient as early as possible, that the paroxysm may not have time to gain strength.

Nightmare Pictures

It's kind of misleading that there are pictures of people experiencing sleep paralysis when the topic is in fact nightmares. Though the two are similar, they're quite different.

As originally defined by Dr.Johnson in his Dictionary and understood by Erasmus Darwin, Henry Fuseli, and others, they are the same
phenomenon. Jclerman 01:17, 4 October 2005 (UTC)

With all due respect, I have experienced nightmares, night terrors, sleep paralysis, lucid dreams, regular dreams, and a large combination of the above. I have researched dreaming, lucid dreaming, nightmares, and insomnia for my psych university studies (as well as for personal interest) read countless articles about dreams and dream-related material and can tell you that sleep paralysis and nightmares are
uncategorically different and that empirical psychological studies recognize them as such. The terms 'sleep paralysis' and 'nightmare' may indeed have had the same meaning at some point in the distant past, but a lot of advances have been made in the area

of dream research over the past 15 years. I really can't stress how incredibly inaccurate it is to use the terms 'sleep paralysis' and 'nightmare' interchangeably. Also, I'm fully confident that our understanding and definition for these two terms have altered somewhat since their initial conception in, what... the 1700's? -- Rathilien 02:54, 3 November 2005 (UTC)

1: I don't believe the terms are currently used interchangeably without qualification. If you find it to be otherwise please quote the place/source for correction/clarification.

2: Please quote references for your other statements, for the information to be incorporated into the article.

Why Two?

Why are their two different versions of the same painting? raptor 13:22, 2 July 2006 (UTC)

Because the artist painted two different versions. 69.9.28.7 13:29, 2 July 2006 (UTC)

Come on, this is not the article for the painting, we don't need a second one. Removed it. 99boy (talk) 05:29, 28 November 2007 (UTC)

Removed Sections

I have removed the following sections because they are copyvios taken from this site. If someone wants to rephrase them to avoid the ©-violation – be my guest. I also added a link to the site, as it was very informative. --Salman 16:22, 6 September 2005 (UTC)

Etymology

The "mare" in "nightmare" is not a female horse, but a mara, an Anglo-Saxon and Old Norse term for a female spirit that sat on sleepers' chests, causing them to have bad dreams.

A nightmare is called a mareridt in Danish, a cauchemar in French, a pesadilla in Spanish, and an Alpdruck or Alptraum in German. The Alp is a demonic being that presses upon sleeping people so that they cannot utter a sound. These attacks are called Alpdrücke (nightmares). In Italian, the word incubo recalls the Incubus, a demon supposed to lie upon sleepers, especially women, and rape them.

Folk Remedies

A folk remedy has it that by stopping up the keyhole, placing one's shoes with the toes facing the door, and then getting into bed backward one can protect oneself against nightmares or "Mortriden." [mare rides]. Or one can put something made from steel, for example, an old pair of scissors, in one's bedstraw. A third remedy suggests that a person suffering from nightmares should urinate into a clean, new bottle, hang the bottle in the sun for three days, carry it—without saying a word—to a running stream, and then throw it over one's head into the stream.

Categorization

I don't want to keep clashing with [User:Jclerman|Jclerman]] here, but categorizing nightmares into Category:Neuroscience is just too broad. In essence, just about any human event can be categorized into "neuroscience". I recategorized this into the more specific Category: Sleep disorders. Semiconscious (talk · home) 09:34, 25 December 2005 (UTC)

The nightmare (and its "menagerie" of the hag, mara, incubus, succubus, and hundred of other "entities" appear to dreamers during episodes of the "nightmare (in the original, i.e. older meaning of the term as used by Johnson, Erasmus Darwin, and Fuseli)" which has been called, by Mary Shelley, "waking dream". It is considered only in a few cases a sleep disorder. Thus the entry under "notes" in the article. Jclerman 10:20, 25 December 2005 (UTC)

We disagree. I'm not sure why you continue to reference Mary Shelley as though she is an expert on the matter of neuroscientific principles. The papers you reference do not have anything to do with the folkloric creature "Nightmare". I've taken this to arbitration, so it's a moot point now. I'm sorry I'm not explaining my self in such a way as to make you truly understand what I'm trying to express. Semiconscious (talk · home) 07:43, 26 December 2005 (UTC)

I must agree with Semiconscious here. There is a fair amount of neuroscientific research into dreaming and nightmares, but if there is a more specific category available it should go there.

I am astounded by how bad this article is. It has almost nothing to do with its subject. Mostly it talks about sleep paralysis (which I probably spelled wrong) which is a different thing (noticeable from the fact that it is called sleep paralysis and not nightmares). This article could be almost entirely scrapped and started over.-- Matt D 19:32, 20 November 2006 (UTC)

I couldn't agree more. As noted above, the article is mostly about Sleep paralysis, which already has its article, and mentions almost nothing about actual nightmares. I vote for getting that tag on the page that says the article needs an expert (Sorry, I don't know Wikipedia enough to know the term...), and having said expert rewrite most if not all of the article. -- Devnevyn 10:35, 25 November 2006 (UTC)

Yet another voice saying this article is complete garbage. Who had the bright idea that the article about "Nightmare" should be about its usage 1-2 centuries ago? The only thing in the entire article that talks about nightmares (current usage) are the introduction! Beyond the etymology of the term, which we will want to keep, the historical usage is the least significant part of any reasonable article. Any other votes for scrapping this article? I'm thinking of dropping it completely would be appropriate. Is there another version out in Wikipedia-land somewhere that might provide real information?

nightmare defined by the M-W online:

nightmare

One entry found for a nightmare.

Main Entry: nightmare

Pronunciation: 'nIt-"mer

Function: noun

Etymology: Middle English, from 1night + 1mare

1. An evil spirit formerly thought to oppress people during sleep
2. A frightening dream that usually awakens the sleeper
3. Something (as an experience, situation, or object) having the monstrous character of a nightmare or producing a feeling of anxiety or terror

Jclerman 05:11, 18 January 2007 (UTC)

I put it there. --Shay Guy 03:28, 18 January 2007 (UTC)

I agree also. In a roundabout way, it discusses something quite different and dated. The whole article is unfocused (at this point-29 Dec 07). Plus, the little linguistic foray in one paragraph which has no place here. I've seen similar things like that be put into other articles and then removed almost unanimously very quickly. Wikipedia is not a translator...

I'm removing this paragraph but leaving it here for later reference if needed. I think this whole article should be scrapped too... Chris b shanks (talk) 18:26, 29 December 2007 (UTC)

Nonsense. The M-W online is not 200 yrs old. The ethnic minorities use those names when describing the waking dreams to their physicians, to their social workers, to the police, etc. The anthropologists use those "translations" when describing the phenomenon in different contemporary cultures. Deleting the article would be a gross mistake. If you can't write a better one, wait for an expert to do it. Jclerman (talk) 11:57, 30 December 2007 (UTC)

Nonsense? It is impolite to address someone that way on Wikipedia. (1)Please see Wiki Policy 'Wikipedia: Wikipedia is not a dictionary,' (and read it) especially the part where it explains, concerning Wikipedia, "Articles are about the people, concepts, places, events, and things that their titles denote. The article octopus is about the animal: its physiology, its use as food, its scientific classification, and so forth." In contrast, Wikipedia is not (but Wiktionary is) "about the actual words or idioms in their title. [In Wiktionary] the article octopus is about the word "octopus": it's part of speech, its pluralizations, its usage, its etymology, its translations into other languages, and so forth." (2) Furthermore, if the reader wants to see what a 'nightmare' is in other languages, they could just CLICK on that language on the left-hand side of the screen then read the title of the article. (3) I have seen such a paragraph get removed from another article with nearly unanimous support (sorry, but I honestly can't remember at this point which article that was) as it is quite unencyclopedic. (4) This is not a specialty 'anthropological' encyclopedia, nor is it an etymological dictionary. (5) Wikipedia is a reference for the average reader, not specifically physicians, social workers, and police looking for translations. (6) If such translations are necessary and important for such professionals using Wikipedia, why does a heavily edited/trafficked page such as rape not have a list of translations into every conceivable another language, which would most definitely be used on a more frequent basis by 'physicians,' 'social workers,' and 'police?' (7) Checking this article's history, other editors have made the same move, only to be reverted by you (e.g. SweetNeo85 on 23 Sept 2006, "Removed unneeded translations"). (8) Finally, on your comment about waiting for an expert-- the history also records that you simply remove the request for expert tags if they're put up (e.g. 17 July 2007), when this article is desperately in need of such help (I don't claim that I'm an expert). Chris b shanks (talk) 02:18, 1 January 2008 (UTC)

As there is no response, I'm removing it again. If we still disagree, we should do a request for a comment. Chris b shanks (talk) 06:34, 12 January 2008 (UTC)

Nightmares: One of The Bodies Defense Mechanisms?

In the instant that I am woken byhaha a nightmare, my first sensation besides panic is of excessive heat. This has become such a noticeable occurance that I can only conclude that the purpose of the nightmare was to wake me up to prevent damage to my body or brain. The cause of the heat was not an illness but external factors, i.e. too many blankets, the heating left on, the cat sleeping on me! Thus, after being woken and feeling hot, I removed the cause of the heat and returned to a peaceful sleep. Are nightmares warnings that our brains are overheating? Is it a biological safety device? The thought intrigues me. Could we be causing the nightmares of our children and babies by trying too hard to keep them warm and tucked in at night? Any thoughts?

While intriguing, this is known as "Original Research" and is not appropriate to include in Wikipedia. If you can get this idea published in a mainstream journal on psychology or neuro-science and if it then becomes notable, then someone else (not you!) could reference it in the article.

---The reason you're waking up is not because of the nightmare but because your body is uncomfortable. You just happen to remember the dream *because* you woke up, not the other way around. If you slept through the nightmare, you would have woken up at your normal time and not remembered the dream. You only remember the dream because you woke up and you woke up for whatever reason, not because of the dream. —Preceding unsigned comment added by 96.232.12.202 (talk) 19:59, 5 January 2009 (UTC)

Dying in A Dream?

"(although not proven, many people believe that dying within a dream is an impossible feat, as there have never been any cases of a person reporting the feelings of the wound or disease that killed them in their dreams)"

I'm not sure what exactly counts as dying in a dream, but I once had a dream in which somebody shot me in my head (good thing it's not a premonition, yet), followed by a brief yet intense pain in my head, after which I began to faint, and my senses weakened rapidly as if fleeing my body. I don't remember anything afterward, which pretty much makes me good as dead. Does anybody else have a similar experience?

Maybe because we don't know what dying is like so our subconscious can't replicate it?

The reason you saw that you were shot in your sleep is that when you get hurt in your sleep the body tries to make a quick explanation for it. When you stub your toe, you don't feel this because you know what happened, but since you are asleep the body will make up a story (if you have a strong imagination) such as being shot. You probably were just dehydrated. —

Rewrite Paragraph

The paragraph under the "Historic Use of term" section that lists the translation of nightmare in 17 different languages is poorly written as just listing information in a paragraph is of bad form. Also, the information to me is arbitrary. In an article that is talking about nightmares, there doesn't need to be translations of the word into multiple languages. So, either this info should go, or it needs to be placed in a small table.

Style is in the brain of the beholder. Moreover, translations should stay. They are not language

translations but anthropologic translations, i.e., they are not strict equivalents but they name the particular regional and/or culturally
dependent demons. Jclerman 03:42, 4 September 2007 (UTC)

Ghost?

Hi, I would just like to know if anyone knows of, or has experienced a ghost pinning them down and not being able to move? Because this morning I woke up at about 5 am but I didn't bother checking the time because for some reason lately, I've been waking up at that exact time a lot. So, I just rolled over and tried to go to sleep, which was weird because it felt like I got to sleep straight away. Then when I think I was changing positions, all of a sudden, I couldn't move, and I was in an uncomfortable position but I was just stuck. I could only move my eyes and maybe head slightly, and as I was all paralyzed, I could see a weird round light skim across the roof of my bedroom. It was like a bright bluish-white color and from my position looked about the size of a tennis ball. So, in this time of me trying to move, I could see it skimming to directly across my head, but as soon as I breathed out help, I felt a release and I could move again and I was awake. This was weird for me and scary as I could remember every vivid detail and it did not even feel like I had gone to sleep, and when I woke, I figured out that this would have happened in no less than 10 minutes of me waking the 1st time. Also, the way I tried crying out for help felt like I was being choked, which I could tell from the sound of my voice. And I also remember consciously thinking at the time as soon as I saw the light of aliens or ghosts, which made it feel like I was awake. I'm still not sure whether I was awake or asleep during this experience. I don't have a lot of nightmares; I can't even remember the last time I did and I didn't watch any scary movies the night before. Can anyone help? TeePee-20.7 08:49, 14 November 2007 (UTC)

You describe the classic nightmare, now usually called sleep paralysis with hypnagogic hallucinations. The term used by Mary Shelley in the intro to Frankenstein is more descriptive: waking dream. You were both awake and dreaming at the same time. See the articles linked above and the references you'll find in them. It's nothing paranormal but normal physiology. Only it happens too frequently it might reflect one of the hypersomnias sleep disorders Jclerman 19:53, 14 November 2007 (UTC)

Oh, ok cool, thanks heaps yeah it sounds like I had one of them. TeePee-20.7 06:03, 15 November 2007 (UTC)

But there is only one thing that bugs me. When you first told me about this type of nightmare after reading the information and seeing that I fitted the criteria of these and had many of the symptoms, I chose to believe that. Not only because I showed the symptoms, but mainly because I was scared and wanted to believe it was this. But just tonight I was watching TV and the channel I was watching had a documentary on aliens, and one of the experiences was very similar to mine which made me remember my own. And which also made me remember the one thing that I chose to ignore and forget about my experience. Why did this all end when I cried my breathless help?

Moving your eyes, especially making vocal noises, will help you get out of sleep paralysis. Happens to me rarely, just do those things and it goes away. That's what happens when you cried your breathless help.69.120.222.239 (talk) 23:39, 23 July 2008 (UTC)

Multivitamins May Be Causing Your Sleep Problems

I don't see a lot of information on the subject of vitamins related to sleep problems but luckily my wife did a lot of research on this (in her own best interest -- she was afraid I might hurt her thrashing around in bed) and she mentioned it to me. I had been taking a multivitamin every day before we were married because I didn't feel that my bachelor's diet was very complete. Thankfully my wife is an excellent cook using plenty of veggies so I stopped the vitamins and my night terrors stopped immediately. Just out of curiosity I even tried taking just a half vitamin in the morning instead of night and the problems returned the same day.

I used to always have a mild to extreme terror about 1.5 hours after going to sleep. I don't know exactly what vitamin/mineral was responsible for this but from what I've seen it could be Magnesium or maybe Vitamin B.

At any rate, if you suffer from Nightmares/Night Terrors do yourself a favor and stop all supplements for a few days and see if it helps.

Good Luck. —Preceding unsigned comment added by 72.42.80.64 (talk) 14:03, 9 September 2008 (UTC)

"Sleep promotes relaxation, and gives us a chance to recuperate and let go of the stresses of the day," says Dr. Natasha Bijlani, a consultant psychiatrist who provides treatment for anxiety at Priory Hospital Roehampton. "However, this isn't the case for the many individuals who struggle with anxiety and panic attacks at night."

There is no single reason why people experience anxiety or panic attacks at night, she explains, but several factors may be involved.

"We do know that the brain doesn't 'switch off' during sleep, so any pent-up worries or anxieties can manifest in our unconscious brains, leading to nocturnal panic attacks," Bijlani says.

Simply being aware that others are sleeping soundly can lead to a sense of isolation and worsen anxiety, too. Small problems, such as forgetting to post a letter, can suddenly seem much worse than they are.

"Those who struggle with daytime anxiety and panic attacks are more likely to experience such symptoms at night because there are fewer distractions to prevent them from worrying excessively and further, their heightened anxiety is likely to affect their quality of sleep," Bijlani explains.

When people are anxious during the day, they can avoid thinking about the thoughts that cause them distress by doing activities, says Nicky Lidbetter, CEO of Anxiety UK. "At night that is harder, and everything is quiet," she says.

Chapter:8

How Neuroplasticity Can Help Overcome Overthinking

One thing that people often misunderstand about Neuroplasticity is that it is always happening. Everything we do changes our brain. Whatever the experience, whether it is an action or a thought, the brain adapts and changes so we get better at that activity and in time it becomes easier than automatic. But all experiences are not 'equal' when it comes to neuroplastic change. Those learnings necessary for survival or where a threat is detected, get priority in brain wiring.

Getting Stuck in Anxiety

Thinking is a brain experience. So, any lingering stressor that we worry over can leave a person with anxiety. Long after the triggering incident has passed (childhood trauma, financial issues, relationship problems, physical illness, work pressures) the echoes of that time can still be found in the wiring of our brain.

Chapter :9

How to Declutter Your Environment to Reflect the Positive Changes You're Making in Your Life

Your Workspace

When your desk is filled with miscellaneous papers, empty coffee mugs, pens that don't work, and a half-eaten granola bar, the clutter in your workspace can harm your productivity.

A workspace with fewer distractions can help you stress less and get more done. You won't have to pause to pick up something that has fallen on the floor. You won't be scrambling to find the document you need when you're on the phone with an important contact.

A clutter-free desk will improve your productivity and time management skills. Take 10 minutes to organize it before work and see how much easier your day becomes.

Your Bedroom

Quality sleep is crucial for staying healthy. By decluttering your bedroom, you will make it a calm area, not a stressful one.

Yes, this means you should make your bed every morning!

Don't let your bedroom become a dumping ground for shoes, dirty laundry, and other various items. Keep your sleeping space sacred so you have a relaxing place to return to after a long, taxing day.

Your Closet

What percentage of clothes in your closet do you wear? If you have a shirt you haven't worn since 2014, it's time to get rid of it.

Consider donating the items you don't wear. People who can't afford to buy clothes could use them. By donating clothing, you are also helping the environment and promoting a sustainable circular economy.

If you have 150 pairs of shoes piling up on the floor of your closet, it's time to downsize so you can improve your quality of life.

Your Desktop

If you've ever run out of disk space, you probably know how much of a toll it takes on the performance of your computer—and a disorganized hard drive makes it so much harder to find crucial files when you need them.

Every file should have a place. Create folders within folders to organize your files, and make sure everything is properly labeled. Uninstall applications you don't use. Make sure the most important items are easily accessible.

Tip: if you need a quick fix, move all your files to an external hard drive so you can sort through them later.

Your Social Media Feeds

The content you consume impacts your mood. Social media should motivate you, not stress you out.

Go through your social media accounts and unfollow accounts that don't inspire you. Don't feel bad—it's not personal. There's so much content out there, and you have every right to balance your media diet.

When you declutter your feeds and become more selective about the content you consume, you'll likely notice a positive change in your mental wellness.

Your Thoughts

Sometimes, the most convoluted clutter lives inside your head. When you get rid of the unnecessary thoughts, you can focus on what matters to you.

If you feel the need to vent, try writing it out in a journal. Or if your to-do list seems unmanageable to the point of overwhelm, it's time to reprioritize.

Accept what you can't change, and work on the things you can change. Make sure you have a little time for relaxation and self-care every day.

The most effective way to declutter your thoughts is to improve your mindset. When you practice gratitude daily and focus on the positive, the little problems in your life won't seem as bad.

Chapter:10

How to Address Information Overload in Your Life

Manage Your Information

Unplugging might not be an option at work, so you're going to have to take another approach. There's an onslaught of information at work but that doesn't mean you have to respond to it immediately when it lands in your inbox.

Be more selective and prioritize your information. When you get an email, most likely you can tell from the subject line whether it needs a quick response or if you can put it aside for a while. Then have a dedicated period during the day in which you can go through your correspondences. Don't forget a spam filter to keep the

171

volume to a reasonable flood. These are key techniques and tools for email management.

Get Everyone Involved

There's only so much you can do on your own in an office. While it's important to control the information that crosses your desk, there is also a more collective data which is beyond your power. You must develop a unified front, and deploy operational excellence, to defeat this invader.

That means creating an information strategy at work. Get buy-in from coworkers, who should be open to any excuse to reduce the exchange of unnecessary information. That could mean keeping paperwork to a minimum and only when essential and keeping meetings on point by having a defined and specific agenda. Of course, upgrading your project management software can help reduce unnecessary steps as well.

Keep It Simple

Information is redundant if it's duplicated. You don't need a carbon copy of everything, and you certainly don't want to get the same notice over and over again. Therefore, do your best to make sure people know how to reach you, so they don't inundate every channel that can get to you to make sure you get their note.

That means, be explicit about whether you prefer email, text or some other form of communication. If they need confirmation, let them tell you so you can respond, rather than having them call you to make sure you've received their missive. It's remarkable how much information a person gets that just says the same thing on a different platform. (If you're running a project, this is where a project communication plan can help clarify how the information will be distributed.)

Clear Your Mind

Think of it as housework. If you don't sweep periodically, you'll have a menagerie of dust bunnies. If you don't clear your head, the important information will have a harder time clearing the hurdles of all that mental debris. Therefore, a regular "brain dump" is a great way to reset your head and keep that pesky information overload at bay.

One way to do this is the old-fashioned way, with pen and paper. Write down every thought that is interrupting your work. It's odd, but once they're on paper, they're out of your head. In a sense, it allows your brain to focus on other things because you've stored information that was blocking it on a paper, the original external hard drive.

Related: Get Inspired: 13 Creativity Exercises for Non-Creatives

Set Limits

There's something called the two-minute rule, which means spending only two-minutes on a task. This is essentially giving yourself limits. One problem with information is that today there is always more and it's easily accessible. From respected sources to anecdotal references, expert advice and commentary to opinions and rants, there's no end to any subject.

But you can put an end to that with this time management strategy. Give yourself boundaries, which citations are valuable, and which are not? Also, how much time is worth the question and when does that time become an impediment to making a decision? Focus on the subject at hand, don't multitask, but give the question the time it deserves and then pull the trigger on the decision.

Prepare for The Next Day

Well, you got through one day without information overload, now it's time to set up the next to be as successful. This should be a daily practice, best to do before you leave work if you're thinking about the office, or before you go to bed if the target is more personal. This focus is a disciplined way to keep information overload under control.

One way to do this is by listing the top few tasks you have to tackle the next day. Prioritize them in a list to collect your thoughts about the coming day, which will also help you not waste time or energy on overthinking the work or being unable to manage it because it's fast becoming due and breathing down your neck.

Was that too much information to take in? Hopefully, it'll prove helpful and make your head clear to handle the day's work. Once you've got the right mindset, then it's time to equip yourself with the right tools. ProjectManager.com is a cloud-based project management software that facilitates workflow with kanban boards, task lists, and a collaborative platform. Manage your information better with

ProjectManager.com by taking this free 30-day trial today.

Conclusion

When you think too much, instead of acting and doing things, you are overthinking. When you analyze, comment and repeat the same thoughts over and again, instead of acting, you are overthinking.

This habit prevents you from taking action. It consumes your energy, disables your ability to make decisions, and puts you on a loop of thinking and thinking over and again.

This is a kind of thinking that wastes your time and energy and prevents you from acting, doing new things and making progress in your life.

It's like tying yourself to a rope that is connected to a pole and going in circles again and again.

In this situation, there is more likelihood of worry, anxiety, and lack of inner peace.

fallacy = eroare
outward = exterior
ironclad = ferit
transgressors = calatori
reclaimed = răscumpărat
to wind up = a sfârși
tackled = a aborda
patterns = modele
reframe = reâncadra
urge = îndemn
assumption = presupunere
cluster = grup
thrust = a împins
swarm = rai
hike = drumeție
flattering = măgulitor, dulce
Gratitude = recunoștință
undo = a anula
berating = jalnic
aware = conștient
fend =
resilient = rezistent